ME AND PAUL

OTHER WORKS BY WILLIE NELSON

Sister, Brother, Family:
An American Childhood in Music

Willie Nelson's Letters to America

Me and Sister Bobbie:
True Tales of the Family Band

Pretty Paper:
A Christmas Tale

It's a Long Story:
My Life

Roll Me Up and Smoke Me When I Die:
Musings from the Road

A Tale Out of Luck

On the Clean Road Again:
Biodiesel and the Future of the Family Farm

The Tao of Willie:
A Guide to the Happiness in Your Heart

The Facts of Life:
And Other Dirty Jokes

Willie:
An Autobiography

ME AND PAUL

Untold Tales of a Fabled Friendship

★

WILLIE NELSON

with David Ritz

HARPER HORIZON

ME AND PAUL

Published by Harper Horizon, an imprint of HarperCollins Focus LLC.

Book design by Aubrey Khan, Neuwirth & Associates, Inc.

ISBN 978-0-7852-4573-5 (Ebook)
ISBN 978-0-7852-4560-5 (HC)

Library of Congress Cataloging-in-Publication Data
Library of Congress Control Number: 2021953427

Printed in the United States of America
22 23 24 25 26 LSC 10 9 8 7 6 5 4 3 2 1

In loving memory of the one and only

PAUL ENGLISH

Me and Paul shaking hands like we did at the end,
every single time we sang our song.
PHOTO BY JANIS TILLERSON

It's been rough and rocky travelin'

But I'm finally standin' upright on the ground

After takin' several readings

I'm surprised to find my mind's still fairly sound

"ME AND PAUL,"
written by Willie in 1971

CONTENTS

A NOTE FROM A GHOST

I'm coming up on my fiftieth year as a ghostwriter. It's a beautiful gig. I've loved collaborating with everyone from Marvin Gaye to Val Kilmer to Cornel West to Janet Jackson to Ray Charles. Each time I've relished the role of being the invisible author.

On this occasion, I've chosen to step forward before turning the story over to Willie. I'm doing so to explain that, unlike *It's a Long Story: My Life*, a previous book I wrote with Willie, *Me and Paul* is not a straight autobiography.

This is something different, a collection of tales—some short, some tall—told by Willie Nelson and his best friend, Paul English. Being in Willie's world for decades, I've spent long hours with both men. In eliciting the essence of their characters, I've taken the poetic license to adorn their stories. As extravagant storytellers themselves, by the way, Paul and Willie freely took that same license.

Novelist Philip Roth argued that one of literature's great lies is that autobiography is built on fact. To paraphrase a quote often attributed to him: memories lie, while fiction should tell the truth. That mixture—of memory and imagination, of fiction and fact—is the key to enduring stories.

Leslie Fiedler, a critic of American literature and a personal mentor, once told me, "Fabulous narratives are all built on the mythic expansion of reality."

I view Willie and Paul as larger-than-life characters who generously and enthusiastically provided me with the stories that constitute this memoir.

Have I embellished those stories?

Yes.

Have I, for the sake of drama, expanded the reality on which those stories were based?

Yes.

Have I tried to give this book a mythic reality of its own?

Yes.

Am I humbled to have been entrusted to work whatever magic great storytelling requires?

Yes.

Have I tried to tap into the extravagant imaginations of Willie Nelson and Paul English?

Yes.

Do I hope that you, our beloved reader, will go along for the ride?

Yes.

Yes.

Yes.

Your ghost,
DAVID RITZ

ME AND PAUL

TEXAS

Present Day

SITTING ON A BEAT-UP LEATHER couch in the study of my ranch outside Austin, listening to my rescue horses whining and feeling the relief of an evening breeze, I find myself lost in thought. In 2020, my closest friend left me. Into the infinite abyss. The mission of this book is to bring him back.

Don't get me wrong. I don't confuse myself with God. I can't resurrect the dead any more than I can turn water to wine. I'm in pretty good shape for someone pushing ninety. I'm at the age when I've long stopped fussing around and started focusing on stuff that matters. Remembering Paul matters. If anyone, Paul must be immortalized. An unlikely drummer. An unlikely angel. If anyone is qualified to tell his story, it's me.

Storytelling is beautiful because it brings people joy. Re-creates life. Turns old reality to new reality. Storytelling reimagines a world from way back when and carries that world into the present day. The people in stories, long dead, get to breathe and speak and laugh and cry all over again. I get to be with those people. I get to hear all that laughing and crying. I get to relive and share those adventures with you.

Why were Paul and I so devoted to each other? Good question. That's another reason I wrote this book—to show the mystical connection between me and Paul. How many people have I met in my life? Hundreds of thousands. Maybe even a million. Preachers, presidents, the rich, the poor, and everyone in between. Yet of those countless folks, this one guy understood me like no one else. He understood me on the deepest level imaginable. Likewise, I understood him. How is it we could communicate without even talking? One look was all we needed. In my case, my only sibling is my sister, Bobbie. Paul became the brother I never had. In Paul's case, he had siblings—wonderfully talented people—and yet our bond felt deeper than blood. It was unbreakable. It defied understanding. It was like I knew him before we ever met. And now that he's gone, he's still here. He still knows me. He still lives in my heart and in the hearts of everyone whose lives he touched.

Another thing about Paul: I owe him big time. The man saved my life more times than I can remember. He did so out of brotherhood. He became my drummer and made a decent living, but hell, if he had stuck to the life he'd been living before he bumped into me, he'd have been a billionaire. Some of the characters Paul knew in his youth, criminal masterminds like Benny Binion, are legendary. Matter of fact, Paul arranged for us to play at Binion's eighty-third birthday party. Binion, who wasn't nearly as crafty as Paul, wound up owning half of Las Vegas and earned status as an iconic gangster.

The purpose of this book is to ensure Paul's iconic status. I'm out to honor him—not because he was perfect but because he was loved. It's been said that a good friend knows all your best stories, but a best friend has lived them with you. Well, that was us.

Picture a towering, larger-than-life human being, a fearless man who, for decades, single-handedly protected me and my band of wandering minstrels from a world that wasn't quite ready for us. In every unsteady situation, Paul stayed steady. Paul stayed strong. In the Willie Nelson Family, he stood in the center. He was the papa bear, the big brother, the wise uncle, the moneyman, the bag man, the dealmaker, the sharpest shooter, and the kindest heart.

Let me start off with a story.

MEMPHIS

1977

THE SIXTEENTH OF AUGUST. Elvis had just dropped dead, and the news swept across the country like wildfire. We were playing Memphis's Mid-South Coliseum, one of the city's biggest venues. Because of Elvis's sudden passing, I was in shock. I'd been an Elvis fan ever since I was a deejay in the 1950s spinning his first hits on KVAN up in Portland/Vancouver. Elvis was a musical giant who showed all us aspiring musicians how to mix and mess with the categories—from country to gospel to rock and roll—and come up with something fresh.

So, there in the city of Graceland, it was an emotional evening. My buddy Delbert McClinton, a singer-songwriter rooted in rhythm and blues, opened the show and, in tribute, sang some of the King's hits. When it was time for me and my band to come on, I took a different approach. I reached back into the Great American Songbook and decided to sing "Over the Rainbow." In thinking of Elvis's untimely passing, that seemed the right sentiment. It also felt right to ask Jerry Lee Lewis up onstage to sing the song with me.

I'd seen Jerry Lee backstage before the show. I had great respect for the man. Along with Elvis, Johnny Cash, and Carl Perkins, he was part of the Million Dollar Quartet recorded by Sun Records—right there in Memphis—that became a musical milestone. Like Elvis, Jerry Lee was a pioneer. Also like Elvis, Jerry Lee started out in gospel. He began with his cousins Jimmy Swaggart, later a famous televangelist, and Mickey Gilley, a friend of mine whose career took off when the movie *Urban Cowboy* was filmed in his club in Pasadena, Texas. For years, Jerry Lee had been a legend. Part of that legend, though, was his nickname, the Killer.

Nine months earlier, Jerry Lee had been arrested outside Graceland. Word came down that he was looking to kill Elvis. Naturally, Jerry Lee denied it. He claimed he was wasted when he crashed into the Graceland gates. Elvis watched it all happening on his closed-circuit TV. His people called the cops, who found a loaded pistol in Jerry Lee's brand-new Rolls-Royce Silver Shadow and hauled him off to jail. Elvis had no problem ordering the officers to lock him up. A few months later, Jerry Lee put out a song called "Middle Age Crazy."

I relay this backstory to let you know what was on my mind when Jerry Lee came to the mic and, instead of harmonizing with me, yelled out to the crowd, "I will be your new king!"

Seeing—and smelling—that Jerry Lee was drunk, I figured I'd better leave well enough alone. I didn't say a word. By then he'd gone to the piano bench, where my sister, Bobbie, was seated, put his arm around her, and started banging away. Bobbie got up and left. Next thing I knew, Jerry Lee was lifting the piano off its legs and slamming it on the floor, all while shouting obscenities at me for reasons I couldn't quite get.

That's when Paul took over.

Paul had my back. Paul always had my back. I mean that in every way possible. He had my back because his drums were behind me, and, like a baseball catcher facing the field in front of him, he saw all the action. But he also had my back no matter where we were—on the bus, at a card game, or prying our pay from some two-timing promoter. He did all this wearing an ensemble that would come to be his signature look: a jet-black suit topped off with a long cape lined in red silk that gave him the demeanor of the devil.

So, on this night of the day that Elvis died, the Killer had to deal with Lucifer's angel himself. Typical of Paul, his action was understated. He did the least to impact the most. In this instance, he reached into his gig bag, pulled out his .45, placed it atop his snare drum, turned to J.W., Jerry Lee's manager, who was standing in the wings, and said, "First, I'm gonna blow your brains out, then I'm gonna shoot Jerry Lee straight through the heart."

Seconds later, J.W. dragged Jerry Lee offstage while I went back to crooning "Over the Rainbow," dedicated to the eternal spirit of Elvis Presley.

No, Paul did not mess around. That's where his power resided. If he said he was gonna do something, he did it. Either you got out of his way or he'd mow you down. You didn't wanna bullshit Paul—not if you valued your life.

But there was a whole lot more to Paul than his wayward proclivities. Underneath the tough guy, he was all heart. He was loyal to the young people who flocked around him like disciples around a guru. Where others were tormented by indecision, Paul was blessed with clarity. He had his own brand of bulletproof morality that won the respect of those he encountered. That is something to admire. It was something I noticed from the very first time we met.

FORT WORTH

1955

MARK TWAIN ONCE SAID, "If you tell the truth, you don't have to remember anything."[1] He's also often credited with having said, "The secret of getting ahead is getting started."

So, I'll heed Twain's words and get started by telling as much of the truth as I can remember. I mention Twain because, as you'll soon see, there's something about my friendship with Paul that reminds me of Tom Sawyer and Huck Finn. Tom was more civilized, and Huck was wilder. Although I was plenty wild at age twenty-two, I'd have to say Paul was wilder. Like Tom and Huck, though, we became a team. Nothing could or would ever separate us. If someone tries to tell my story without putting Paul by my side, don't bother reading it.

★

Let me paint the picture. I was living smack-dab in one of the most boring decades in American history. Except I wasn't bored. I had a job at radio station KCNC. I even had a tagline: I was "your old cotton-pickin', snuff-dippin', tobacco-chewin', stump-jumpin', gravy-soppin', coffeepot-dodgin', dumplin'-eatin', frog-giggin' hillbilly from Hill County, Texas."

I beat back boredom by hustling. And whenever I could, I aligned my hustle with music. If I couldn't hustle up a job playing and singing somewhere, the next best thing was to hustle up a deejaying job. That tagline, by the way, was true.

I did come from the tiny town of Abbott, the heart of Hill County, and I had picked cotton and all the rest. If you called me a hillbilly, you wouldn't be wrong, and I wouldn't be mad. I couldn't ever stay mad at anyone for long—and still can't, by the way—because music takes up so much space inside my head, and music makes me happy. Even in the super-conformist 1950s, music—great music—was everywhere. Elvis went on TV for the first time on the program *Louisiana Hayride*, and shortly after "Heartbreak Hotel" and "Hound Dog" were racing up the charts. This was also the year when you could buy a loaf of bread for a quarter and a gallon of gas for twenty-nine cents. I know because I also pumped gas. The *Fort Worth Star-Telegram* cost a nickel, but who wanted to buy the paper when all the news was about Joe McCarthy, a paranoid asshole who saw commies hiding under every bed in the house? Better to stick with music.

Better to hang out with great musicians, namely my big sister, Bobbie, who'd moved to Fort Worth where she was among the first in the city to play the spanking-new version of the Hammond B3 organ. I'd also befriended Paul Buskirk, who, like Bobbie, was a genius-level player. He knew the work of my guitar hero, Django Reinhardt, note for note. Buskirk's main instrument was banjo, but he could play anything. He was on a TV show on Channel 5 in Dallas with Freddy Powers, a singer who, like me, had studied the records and shows of Bob Wills & His Texas Playboys—the kings of western swing. Bobbie, Buskirk, and Freddy were huge influences because they knew, played, and combined so many styles of music—everything from country to jazz to crooners like Bing Crosby. Together we'd listen to Ernest Tubb or Duke Ellington or Chet Atkins or Bill Haley & His Comets, rockin' around the clock. They didn't discriminate. They didn't care about categories. Music was either good or bad, exciting or dull, fun or flat.

KCNC wasn't much more than a couple of windowless rooms with primitive equipment. The space was tight. The show was called *The Western Express*, where, in addition to playing records, I played live. Sometimes Buskirk and Freddy accompanied me. While they were on the air, I was content to help promote the songs Buskirk was putting out on a little label called Lin. I was more than content when Buskirk had Freddy record a song I'd just written called "Heartaches of a Fool." We never found anyone to release it, but I was still thrilled to hear it sung by a singer as good as him. As a writer, my confidence was on the upswing.

Paul Buskirk and Freddy Powers weren't the only two musicians who came by KCNC. A drummer named Tommy Roznosky and a guitarist named Oliver English were also in the mix. Like Buskirk, Oliver wasn't just a virtuoso; he was a scholar. He taught me about Spanish guitarists like Andrés Segovia and jazz guitarists like Charlie Christian. A Fort Worth native, Oliver had jammed in every club you could name, from the buckets of blood to the fancy ballrooms. As a white guy, he was so great he got a pass to play at the downtown Black hotel, the New Gem, where he sat in with beboppers who were knocked out when they heard him riffing over lines written by Charlie Parker, Dizzy Gillespie, and Thelonious Monk.

Sometimes Oliver would talk about his granddad, who, back in the day, was considered the finest fiddler in Texas, even better than Bob Wills. Oliver did more than play guitar; he *made* guitars. He bent the wood in the bathroom. He sculpted the instruments by hand. And he learned to electrify the guitar and use a television set as an amplifier. Oliver was a certified genius.

He also had a brother whom he brought over to the station. It was Oliver who made the introduction.

"Willie Nelson, meet Robert Paul English. He goes by Paul."

"Hey, man, I thought you were a lot older," Paul said in his nasal Texas twang.

"Why do you say that?" I asked.

"Listening to you on the radio, you sound older. Hearing you sing, you also sound older."

"How am I supposed to take that?"

"Take it as a compliment," big brother Oliver said.

"I meant it as a compliment," Paul added. "You sound like a guy who's been around and has something real to write about."

"Well," I joked, "I been to Waco and Waxahachie."

"Willie's being modest," Oliver said. "He's been to Eugene, Oregon. He was a big star on the radio up there."

"More of a big bust," I added. (I'd been a deejay in Eugene when I'd gone to visit my mom, but then my ratings tanked, and I wound up working as a plumber's assistant.)

"Looks like you're doing all right in Fort Worth," Paul said with genuine encouragement.

"Are you a musician like your brother and granddad?" I asked.

"More a bookkeeper like my dad," Paul explained. He said that his father had also been a clerk at the county courthouse.

Mr. English, who started off in pre-typewriter times, had perfect calligraphy. Later he became a machinist at Convair, the aeronautical giant that turned into General Dynamics and Lockheed. He and his wife, both Pentecostal Christians, had four talented children: Oliver, Paul, Nadine, and Billy.

"A bookkeeper." Oliver smiled. "Paul, give the man your real story."

"You mentioned Waxahachie," Paul whispered with a twinkle in his eye. "I'm not allowed down there no more."

"Why is that?"

"Got myself into some trouble."

"What kinda trouble?"

"Running a craps game."

I had a soft spot in my heart for guys who ran craps games.

As a kid growing up, my best buddy, Zeke Varnon, ran craps games all over Hill County. He was a dominoes champ and a card shark. Zeke was six years older than me. Paul was only six months older but, in some ways, reminded me of Zeke. He lived outside the law. Decades later, Bob Dylan said, "To live outside the law, you must be honest."[2] That describes both Zeke and Paul.

Paul was long, lean, and lanky. When we started talking, he was also candid. Nothing to hide. Like Huck Finn, he was a free soul, eager for and unafraid of any adventure that might come his way.

"As a young teenager, I was arrested a hundred times," he told me. He also said he'd made the *Fort Worth Press*'s Top Ten Most Unwanted Criminals list five years in a row. He wasn't boasting. Just explaining what he'd been doing with his life.

He said, "Whenever there was a murder, the cops would come and ask, 'Where's Paul?' If I wasn't there, the cops always made the same remark: 'He must have just left.' They linked me to three murder trials, but none of them stuck. The only one where I was out-and-out accused happened when six of us were in a shoot-out. Me and my buddies had been cheated at cards, and I wasn't about to let the cheaters get away. One of those cheaters got hit when he ran out of bullets. Well, that's not murder—not in Texas anyway. The jury agreed, and I was set free as a bird. Later I learned to pick locks. That's how I wound up in a Waxahachie jail cell. But I picked that lock too. They never bothered to recapture me because they didn't think I was worth it. The way I made real money was running willing women. Good work, but hard work. Ran it like a regular business. Fixed it with certain hotels so that customers could charge the ladies as an entertainment expense. Might have been the first guy, at least in Texas, to make that arrangement."

You might ask: Why would I decide to trust this guy with my entire life?

My answer is easy: I liked him. Liked being around him. Liked his gutsy outlook on life. Liked that he was razor-sharp and the best damn storyteller I'd ever met. His rebellious streak brought out mine. Paul made me braver, more willing to take chances, more ready to tackle life's big challenges. Instinct rarely steers you off course.

Paul also really appreciated my music. His brother Oliver—ten times the musician I'll ever be—must have also told Paul that I had a future as a singer or writer.

The fact that I was quite literally a Sunday school teacher at the Metropolitan Baptist Church at the time (and also a salesman of the *Encyclopedia Americana* and Kirby vacuum cleaners) didn't mean I looked down on anyone who was off the beaten path. I was interested in the whole wide world, and the world of Fort Worth—especially its underworld—was downright fascinating. In that world, twenty-three-year-old Paul English was already a legend.

If Dallas had ambitions to be high-class, Fort Worth didn't give a damn about all that. That's another thing I liked about Paul. He was Fort Worth to the core. *Regret* wasn't part of his vocabulary. My tiny hometown, Abbott, was agricultural. I was a country boy. Paul was a city boy who'd grown up with the kind of gangsters I'd only read about in books. When we met, I'd already had a good taste of Cowtown culture.

I'd grown up on westerns. My heroes were Gene Autry, Roy Rogers, Lash LaRue, and Whip Wilson. They sang, played guitar, and got the girls. But that didn't mean that I hated the bad guys. No, sir. The cattle rustlers, card sharks, and gunslingers who tore up the saloons made those movies fun. Without them, the heroes couldn't be heroes. Sometimes the guys on the wrong side of the law were more interesting than the heroes themselves.

That's why I found Fort Worth, a city I called Honky Tonk Central, a scintillating scene. It smelled of the Old West. It claimed to be "Where the West Begins." Slaughterhouses over here. Whorehouses over there. A section south of downtown called Hell's Half Acre where hell was raised every night of the week. Even more hell was happening on the Jacksboro Highway, a six-mile strip on the north side heading toward Wichita Falls. Some called it Thunder Road. Others called it the Highway to Hell. I got to know it well because that's where live music was pouring out of a long lineup of nightclubs, restaurants, and motels. Some of those places were fancy, some nasty. It was anything goes, so that's where I went.

When I arrived, things were turning a little seedy. The old-timers told me about the glory days when Sinatra sang at the

Showboat with Tommy Dorsey and the big bands of Benny Goodman and Harry James played the Skyliner. In my day, there were still a few fancy joints, but, if I was lucky, I got a gig at a barroom called the Bloody Bucket.

Paul knew these places like the back of his hand. That day we met at the studio, he asked me if I'd heard of the City Dump. I hadn't.

"It's over on Handley Drive," he said. "You know why it's called the City Dump?"

"Nope."

"Cause it's next to the city dump. You don't wanna play there."

"Cause of the smell?"

"Cause of that thing that happened a few months back."

"What happened?"

"A cowboy shouted out some song he wanted the band to play. When the band didn't play it, the dude pulled out his pistol and shot up the joint."

"Anyone hurt?"

"Only the guitarist."

"How bad?" I asked.

"Well, if you wanna see for yourself, he's over at the morgue."

This was no joking matter, but the way Paul told the story, you had to laugh.

"Something like that wouldn't happen to me," I said.

"Why's that?" Paul asked.

"I'd play any song the cowboy wanted to hear."

"Are we gonna play anything tonight?" Paul's brother Oliver asked as he started tuning his guitar.

"I'm missing a drummer," I said.

"Paul's a musician," Oliver said. "He plays trumpet. And he can also keep time."

"Unlike myself," I admitted. "Get that carboard box over there, Paul, and grab some brushes. I think I have a snare somewhere."

"Don't I need more than a snare?" Paul asked.

"I reckon there's an old Salvation Army bass drum around here as well," I said.

Paul found the drum in the closet along with a set of bongos.

"There's no stool," Paul said.

"Sit on that wooden Coke box," I said.

Paul looked a tad uncomfortable but determined.

"Just let Willie lead you," Oliver said. "Wherever he goes, you go."

Oliver's instructions proved prophetic. Paul was able to follow my spur-of-the-moment musical meanderings. That's no easy task, but Paul was up to it. It came to him naturally.

When we got through, I turned to him and gave a nod of appreciation. He nodded back. That was the first of our meaningful silent conversations. Over our lifetime together, we'd have millions.

It felt good having Paul around—so good that for the next month, he became my drummer on *The Western Express*. That's about when I started singing "Red Headed Stranger," a song I first heard sung by Arthur "Guitar Boogie" Smith. I'd sing it for my baby daughter, Lana, who was at home listening to the radio with her mama, Martha, a high-spirited, full-blooded Cherokee who'd become my wife three years prior. She was a carhop, a waitress at a Waco burger joint. She was sharp as a tack and drop-dead gorgeous. Was she spoiled? Hell yes, but so was I. Was she stubborn? No more than me. I was broke, but she didn't care. Martha made more money than me, a situation that lasted longer than I care to remember. Mainly, though, we couldn't stay away from each other. I loved Martha—loved all my wives with all my heart—although, in the case of Martha, I can't say for sure whether we spent more time fighting or making up. It was a close call.

That "Red Headed" song got to me because it was a cowboy story about a man's wandering ways. The character is "wild in his sorrow," a man you better not boss or cross, fight or spite, because he's "ridin' and hidin' his pain." I related, not just because of the color of the hero's hair but because of his restless spirit.

Playing behind me, Paul felt that spirit. A virtuoso drummer would have done a lot more, would have put in all sorts of accents and added a whole lot of flare. But flare and accents weren't what I needed. I needed someone willing to go on that journey with me, not too fast, not too slow, pause when I felt like pausing, and then get back on the trail when it was time to move on. It wasn't anything I had to teach Paul. No explanations were needed. He could feel the offbeat rhythms and rhymes of the Red Headed Stranger. He could feel the beat of my heart.

KCNC didn't give me any money for the musicians who played on the show, but when I was hired at Major Joe's, I could pay Paul eight bucks a night. That's when we really got to know each other.

Major Joe's was another hole-in-the-wall on one of the highways to hell that crisscrossed the city. Back then, there were big-time venues for country music—the Big D Jamboree in Dallas and the All-Star Country Road Show in the Fort Worth North Side Coliseum. Those were places where thousands thronged to hear Elvis sing "Don't Be Cruel" and Gene Vincent & His Blue Caps do "Be-Bop-A-Lula." At Major Joe's we'd be lucky to get a couple dozen paying customers. A couple dozen, though, could cause a small riot, which was why we were protected by a sheet of chicken wire strung up in front of the bandstand.

As it turned out, I didn't need protection from someone looking to launch a beer bottle. I needed protection from one of my many fascinations: women. I loved smart women, witty women, and shapely women. I was especially vulnerable to women who showed an interest in me before I made the slightest move. I found that exciting. Most musicians will admit that getting girls is a main motivation for going onstage. Ladies like men who make pretty music.

As a young man, I took my marriage vows seriously—but seriousness had its limits. I told myself I wouldn't go chasing, but what if someone chased me? And what if that someone happened to have the sultry eyes of Ava Gardner and the body of Bettie Page? What was a man to do?

In front of a few dozen dancers, I was standing up there picking my guitar and singing "Don't Rob Another Man's Castle," recorded by Eddy Arnold. My favorite version was by Ernest Tubb, who recorded the song with the Andrews Sisters. Of course, I wasn't thinking all that much about the lyrics, which even quote the Bible about "thou shall not steal." Stealing wasn't on my mind. This gal was. She had long brown hair and was wearing a blouse and blue jeans that had to be two sizes too small. She was a lot to look at. The more I looked her way, the more she looked at me. Her bright smile seemed to be saying *yes, yes, yes* as she swayed to the music, twirling around and around to give me a 360-degree view. The closer I came to the mic, the closer she came to the bandstand. Best of all, she danced alone.

"Is that lady flashing me the green light," I asked Paul after we played our last song for the night, "or am I crazy?"

"You're not crazy," Paul offered.

I figured I'd best obey the traffic signs and get going. She was ready. I can't remember her name, and even if I did, I wouldn't tell you. Discretion is important. That night I thought I was being discreet when she approached me. I simply shook her outreached hand.

"I don't stay far from here" was all she said while slipping me a matchbook from the Landmark Lodge Motel over on Highway 80. On the back she had written "Room 12."

Then she turned and headed for the door. She walked slowly, giving me time to take in the view.

"What do you think?" I asked Paul, showing him the matchbook.

"Careful not to get a speeding ticket driving out there."

I packed up my guitar and made my way in a borrowed car. It was late September. The long summer heat had finally given way to what we call football weather. I thought back to those times in Abbott when we roughed it up on a rocky field. As a kid, I played all the sports. I liked contact sports. Driving through the night, I couldn't help but think that romance was a contact sport. This little lady was dying for contact. And I wasn't one to deny her.

I passed by the Coyote Drive-In where they were showing a double feature of *East of Eden* and *The Seven Year Itch*. I could see dozens of cars parked in front of the giant screen, but hardly a head was visible. One two-toned Packard Clipper was bumping up and down something fierce. Might have been the full moon. Might have been the starlit sky. But Fort Worth looked mighty pretty. Even the pawn shops. Even the liquor stores. Even the junkyards. Everything had its own charm. The big neon sign in front of the Landmark Lodge let you know that they had air coolers, televisions, and a swimming pool. It wasn't a dump. My new friend was sitting in the lobby. She saw me pull up and started walking to room 12. I followed and was able to park right in front.

"You gonna bring in your guitar so I can hear you sing a little more?" she asked.

"I never refuse requests," I answered.

She had a candle placed on a table beside the bed. When she lit it, the smell of lavender filled the room. She was drinking out of a bottle of Bellows Bonded Bourbon and offered me a swig. I accepted. Neither of us was feeling any pain. She sat on the edge of the bed. Always trying to comport myself in a gentlemanly manner, I knew better than to move too fast. We had all night.

I sat in an easy chair in the corner, took out my guitar, and started to strum.

"I got a request," she said, "but it's a corny one."

"I don't mind corn."

"You know 'Deep in the Heart of Texas'?"

"I'd be a damned fool if I didn't."

As I started singing about stars at night being big and bright, prairie skies being wide and high, sage in bloom smelling like perfume, the lady took her time. One button at a time, she undid her blouse. Inch by inch, she unzipped and stepped out of her jeans. She reclined on the bed, a sight to behold.

I put down my guitar, but she wanted to hear more.

"This time something real romantic," she said.

Singers sing for their supper, so I had no problem accommodating. I was a patient man.

"What's your favorite romantic tune?" I asked.

"What's yours?"

I answered with "A Sinner Kissed an Angel," a song Frank Sinatra had sung when he was with the Tommy Dorsey

Orchestra. For all my love of the country music heroes—Jimmie "The Singing Brakeman" Rodgers, Hank Williams, Hank Snow, Ray Price, and all the rest—Sinatra was my favorite singer. There was something about his phrasing. He had that eighteen-karat-gold longing in every word. His voice was his heart.

As I sang, my friend closed her eyes and leaned back. I strummed the last chord and was ready—finally ready—to embrace all that bliss when we were both startled by a thunderous knock on the door and a man's voice yelling, "Who you got in there with you?" The man didn't sound friendly.

The lady jumped off the bed and put on a robe.

"What are *you* doing here?" she asked. "You said you were going back to Denton."

"Changed my mind and turned around."

"Why?"

"Smelled something fishy. Now open the door. Whoever's in there with you better kiss his sweet ass goodbye."

"No one's in here."

"I heard music."

"That was the radio."

"Wasn't no radio. If you got another one of those pickers in there, he's a dead man."

All the time he was saying this stuff, he kept banging, banging, banging until I was sure he'd break down the door. Though I wasn't the kind of guy who'd always back down from a fight, especially when fueled by liquor, I was hardly prepared. I looked around the room to see what might be available—A razor blade? A penknife?—but all I could spot was a pencil advertising Mrs. Baird's bread. Not exactly my weapon of choice.

The lady had run into the bathroom and locked the door, leaving me to my lonesome, when her caller—Her husband?

Her boyfriend?—kicked in the door. He looked to be my age, somewhere in his early twenties, but that's where the resemblance stopped. I was thin; he was thick. I was short; he was tall. He was holding a pistol; I wasn't. His eyes were so red I expected to see flames shooting out.

My options were limited. I could try to charge him, but that would be suicide. I could try to jump out the window over the bed, but that would also be suicide. I could beg him for my life, but I wasn't the begging type. I could try to reason with him, but reason wasn't on my side.

"Do you know who you were just screwing with?" he asked.

"Wasn't screwing anyone. Hadn't had time."

"Then do you know who you were about to screw?"

"A lady I met at a bar."

"That's my fiancée."

He took a step closer and aimed his pistol at my crotch.

"I'm blowing off your balls," he said.

"*Not if I slice your wrist first.*"

That last voice wasn't mine. It was Paul's. He was standing behind the dude with a Smith & Wesson twelve-inch carbon killer blade pushed just hard enough into the back of the man's right wrist to draw a drop of blood.

My assailant put down his gun.

"Grab your guitar," Paul said to me, "and let's scram."

That's just what we did.

★

An hour later we were down on Taylor Street sitting on a bench at Bailey's BBQ chewing on brisket and greasy fries. Best meal of the week.

Aside from thanking Paul, I hadn't said much. Neither had he. We were both more interested in eating than talking.

That's how it was between me and Paul. It was always good timing. I can't explain it. Don't want to explain it. Mysteries are mysteries because they can't be solved. Otherwise, you'll ruin the mystery. The mystery between me and Paul had to do with us always being in the right place at the right time. I didn't tell him to show up at that motel seconds before I was about to get my nuts blown to bits. He just sensed that I needed backup.

When he started drumming behind me, he had no experience. That made it better 'cause he worked on instinct. He knew, musically speaking, that I moved on instincts that were unpredictable. He soon saw that was also how I led my life, moving from one city to another at quirky times for quirky reasons. Paul knew not to ask why. That's because he knew *I* didn't know why.

Understanding without explaining is a hell of a thing between two human beings. It wasn't that me and Paul weren't curious about each other. We were. And it wasn't that we didn't respect each other. We did. It's just that we knew not to fret about our pasts or worry about the future. Paul was a right-here-and-now kinda guy. Life was never about tomorrow or yesterday. It was about sitting at Bailey's BBQ and digging into the brisket.

We washed down the meal with mugs of black coffee.

After long minutes of silence, Paul said one word: "Women."

He didn't say it disparagingly. He just said it. Then he repeated it.

"Women."

"What about 'em?" I asked.

"Damn few men have them figured out."

"How about you?"

"Nope. I come from a place where the women were mainly looking to get married."

"Where's that exactly?"

"Born in Harrold just outside Vernon. You know where Vernon is?"

"West of Waco by the Red River."

"That's right."

"That's a big place compared to where I grew up."

"Thought you were from Dallas."

"Nope," I said. "Abbott. Twenty-five miles north of Waco. Population five hundred."

"I figured you as big city."

"You figured wrong. And I figured you as a Fort Worth slicker."

"I been here most of my life, but I'm not all that slick. I messed up early and hard."

"How?"

"Spent nine months in jail when I was seventeen."

"What'd you do?"

"Didn't understand women. One in particular. She was ten years older. Showed me things I'd never seen before. Things I'd never imagined before. She turned me inside out. Had me feeding out of her hand. Told me about these rich folks who were out of town. Talked me and a buddy into going by their house and breaking in. I chickened out. I stayed in the car while my buddy slipped through a window. He was so scared he didn't do much more than raid the refrigerator. No money, no jewelry, and a no-good 1942 Nash that crapped out just as we were pulling away. Here come the cops. Here comes the court date. Here comes the twenty-dollar lawyer hired by my dad. Here comes the sentence. Nine months."

"Sitting in a cell?"

"Working the fields. Picking peas."

"I liked working the fields."

"So why you out here then?"

"Music's in my bloodstream."

"I can see that. And I can see what music does to the women. That must be good for your bloodstream as well."

I smiled. Paul nodded. He took out his pack of Lucky Strikes and offered me one. We smoked in silence, the smell of strong tobacco filling the air. We took our last puffs and went back for more coffee.

Paul was still toying with that old memory. "Back there in jail," he said, "I learned more than how to pick peas. Old-timer set me straight. Said, 'If you gonna be a thief, you can be the best thief in the world, but you best plan on spending most of your life in jail. If you wanna make real money and keep your young ass out of jail, get into the rackets. You'll wind up dealing with a better class of people.'"

"And that's what you've done?"

"So far. But I got other interests. Me and Oliver just bought a used car lot over on North Main."

"Oliver never mentioned that."

"Oliver don't want you to get messed up in my schemes. He sees you as Mr. Music."

"Oliver is Mr. Music, not me. Oliver can play. I play at it."

"You play at it good. Singing. Leading a band. Charming the ladies."

"Which isn't easy if you don't have a car."

Paul gave me a funny look.

"You want a car?"

I sighed. "Who doesn't?"

"You trust me?"

"Yeah."

"Enough to sell you a car?"

"Why not?"

"There are no bigger thieves than used-car salesmen."

"You just told me you swore off thieving early on."

Paul smiled and sipped. “You like convertibles?” he asked.

“Who doesn’t?”

“Got a 1946 Buick. Jet-black with bloodred upholstery. One owner. You can have it for a hundred and seventy-five bucks.”

“I don’t have that much cash on hand,” I said.

“I’ll sell it to you on time. Twenty-five bucks down, the rest when you can. What do you say?”

“I say yes.”

“Sight unseen?”

“Sight unseen.”

Paul offered his hand, and I shook it with zeal.

The Buick turned out to be a beauty. I later learned that only a week earlier the car had cost Paul $250.

Paul (left); his brother Billy (back), who is now Willie's drummer; Paul's older brother, Oliver (right); and Willie (front and center).

DALLAS

Shortly Thereafter

THE FIRST SHORT TRIP I took in that Buick was with Paul. It was a Saturday night when we drove over to Dallas to see about hustling up some gigs. The Bob Wills Ranch House, on Corinth Street in the industrial wastelands south of downtown, was the biggest music barn in the city. When we walked in, Paul introduced me to a man standing by the front door. In his gray suit, white shirt, and black bow tie, the man looked out of place. Everyone else was wearing working clothes, overalls, and jeans. Some of the gals were wearing cowgirl getups. Most of the fellas had cowboy hats. This guy was smoking a pipe.

"Willie," Paul said, "meet O. L. Nelms."

Well, I'd heard of O. L. Nelms because he'd plastered giant billboards from here to Fort Worth saying, "Thanks to All of You for Helping O. L. Nelms Make Another Million." Nelms was the real estate mogul who owned the Bob Wills Ranch House. He named it after Wills because they were buddies.

"How you are you doing, Paul?" asked Nelms.

"Fair to middlin'," Paul answered.

How in hell did Paul know O. L. Nelms? Short answer: Paul knew everyone.

Hank Snow was onstage singing his big hit "Cryin', Prayin', Waitin', Hopin'." Miss Kitty Wells was on the same show. We hung around to hear her do "It Wasn't God Who Made Honky Tonk Angels." I've always liked Kitty. A few years later, I'd go back to this same place after it was renamed the Longhorn Ballroom. That's when Dewey Groom, a singer himself, took it over from Nelms and devoted one night a week to Black blues. Paul also knew Dewey. Many were the times me and Paul went over there to hear great artists like B. B. King, Freddie King, and Bobby "Blue" Bland.

Naturally, Nelms wasn't about to hire a nobody like me to play his Ranch House. Paul had other promoters in mind. We headed into the heart of downtown where, across the street from the fancy Adolphus Hotel, was Abe Weinstein's Colony Club. If a strip joint could be called classy, the Colony Club fit the bill. This time we went through the back door, straight to Abe's office. A thin-faced man with a five o'clock shadow, Abe wore a double-breasted suit and black fedora. He was hunched over an open ledger on his desk. When he looked up, he seemed pleased to see Paul.

"I wish I had your dad doing my books," Abe said. "He'd do a better job than me."

"Abe knew my dad," Paul told me. "Dad was the best accountant in the state."

After introducing me, Paul asked Abe whether he'd ever listened to my *Western Express* radio show. He hadn't. He and his brother, Barney, owned a bunch of clubs, but according to Abe, they didn't want country music.

"Can Willie play bump-and-grind music?" asked Abe.

"Willie can play anything."

"I'm sure he can, but right now I don't have a thing."

"Nothing ventured, nothing gained," Paul said. "Mind if we take a peek inside?"

"Be my guest."

The club was awash in red—red brocade wallpaper, red leatherette banquettes, waitresses in skin-tight red skirts. The red curtains were drawn, and Shari Angel, billed as "The Girl with the Heavenly Body," came out in a G-string and pasties. In those days, that was as far as they'd let the gals go.

We stood in a corner watching. Abe joined us for a minute.

He asked Paul, "What do you think?"

Paul gave a small nod.

"Glad you approve," Abe said. "Next week we're bringing Candy Barr back. You don't want to miss Candy. Jack Ruby tried to book her, but she turned him down flat. The guy's a bum. Stay away from Jack Ruby."

A minute or so after leaving the Colony Club, Paul said, "Let's go see Jack Ruby."

I had to laugh.

We walked down Akard Street where Paul pointed out four or five other strip clubs.

"Jack Ruby owns a couple of these," he said. "The Weinstein brothers hate his guts, but Jack has connections. No reason not to pay Jack a visit."

At the corner of Commerce and Ervay, we bumped into David "Fathead" Newman, a handsome Black man with an easy smile and thick mustache. A Dallasite, Fathead played sax in Ray Charles's band. He was also Ray's best friend. I was crazy for Ray's music. "I Got a Woman" had just come out, and even on my country music show, I'd play the thing every chance I got. Paul and I had gone to see Ray's band in a club on Jacksboro Highway. We hadn't met Ray personally, but we knew Fathead, a friendly gentleman.

"We're looking for Ruby," Paul told Fathead. "You seen him?"

"He was just here. Matter of fact, we had a run-in."

"What happened?" Paul asked.

"Well, I was playing in a band at his place . . ."

"How come?" I asked.

"Ray's off the road for a couple of weeks," Fathead said. "I wanted to pick up a few extra bucks. Easy gig. Except with Jack, nothing's easy. He accused me of looking at the strippers while I was playing."

"I don't get it," I said.

"Jack was bitching about how his white clientele don't want to see a Black cat drooling over a naked white chick. But that don't make sense. His white clientele is looking at Chris Colt and her forty-fives. They can't keep their eyes off her forty-fives. No one is looking at me. And I'm just looking to get through this dumbass gig and split."

"He fire you?" Paul asked.

"I quit," Fathead said. "Should have never taken the gig. You ever know Zuzu Bollin?"

"I knew Zuzu," Paul said. "Blues guy."

"Had a big hit. Or what should have been a big hit. 'Why Don't You Eat Where You Slept Last Night?' After the record came out, Ruby hired Zuzu to play at one of his clubs. After a week of packed crowds, Zuzu got half of what he was promised. Zuzu called Ruby a scumbag. Then Ruby got the deejays to stop playing Zuzu's record. That was the beginning and end of Zuzu."

"Well, at least you got your gig with Ray. When are you guys going out again?" I asked.

"Not sure. Ray just moved here."

"Ray Charles is living in Dallas?!"

"South Dallas," Fathead said. "Over on Eugene Street. You should come over and say hello."

"Always wanted to meet him," I said. "Wonder what he's like in everyday life."

"You play chess?" Fathead asked.

"Yes indeed," Paul said.

That surprised me. I was a chess player myself. Didn't figure Paul as one.

"Well, that's the opening," Fathead said. "Ray's always looking for good chess players."

"Meanwhile," Paul said, "where do you think we can find Ruby?"

"Probably over at his place in Oak Lawn."

★

A big neon sign said "Lucas B&B," an all-night ham-and-eggs eatery. Me and Paul parked right in front. Next door was the Vegas Club, Jack Ruby's after-hours spot. I'd passed by it before when Bobbie and I had gone to church where she played organ for Sunday services. The church was in Highland Park, a highfalutin neighborhood of huge mansions right around Oak Lawn.

The dance floor was crowded, the smoke was thick, and music was coming from a loudspeaker, playing Jimmy Reed blues. The band was on break. A back room had paintings of bosomy women on the wall. Real-life bosomy women were working two different roulette wheels. Green felt tables were set up for poker and blackjack. I was tempted, but I was broke. Beyond the back room was an office with blue velvet walls and a white wood desk. The stocky man seated behind the desk had beady eyes, thin lips, slicked-back dark hair, a white boutonniere in the lapel of his silk suit, and a cigarillo in his mouth.

"Meet Jack Ruby," Paul said, making the introductions.

Ruby seemed happy to see Paul. It seemed like everyone was happy to see Paul. You felt good being around him. And if he was your friend—like he was to so many people—you also felt safe.

"Either you got something for me," Ruby said with a distinct Chicago accent, "or you want something from me."

"What would I have for you?" Paul asked.

"A dame. Two dames. Three dames. What do I know? You tell me, Paul."

"Not into that kind of operation these days."

"So where are you working?"

"Working with this guy." Paul nodded in my direction.

"What does he do?" Ruby asked.

"Sings. Plays. Writes. Got his own radio show."

"How's that gonna make me any money?"

"He's really good," Paul said. "His band is lighting up Fort Worth."

"Fort Worth is a hillbilly town. Farmer's town. Pigsty town. This here is different. You saw the name out front? This here is more Vegas, more Monte Carlo. Whatever gets over in Fort Worth falls flat in Dallas."

"How many spots you got, Jack?" Paul asked.

"I got what used to be the Singapore Supper Club. I renamed it the Silver Spur Club. I also got Hernando's Hideaway. I used to have the Bob Wills Ranch House."

"We saw Nelms over there tonight," Paul said.

"Nelms stole it from me. I'll get it back. I'll also get the Weinsteins. I got plans to open a swank club that'll put their Colony out of business. You hit them up for work?"

Paul gave one of his coy little nods. "Abe sends his regards."

"Abe can go to hell. Him and his brother Barney both. Small-time operators."

"They got big-name entertainers."

"They got big-time shit. They're small-time schmucks."

"Well," Paul said, seeing we were getting nowhere, "you know where to find me."

"Find me some dames," Ruby said. "Dames were your thing. You always did good with the dames. Better leave this Willie fella alone and stick with what you know."

★

Eggs over easy, home fries, crisp bacon, buttermilk biscuits. Me and Paul in a booth at Lucas B&B wolfing down a late-night breakfast. The fluorescent lights were buzzing. I felt a little buzzed myself from the beers and whiskey I'd been drinking at our various stopovers while Paul remained stone-cold sober. A plate of hot food did me good.

I asked Paul more about his history with women.

"I had a lady working for me a few years back," he explained. "I'd barely turned twenty-one, and so had she. She needed protection. I needed money. She had friends interested in the same line of work. I set up shop at the Western Hills Inn way out in Euless. Low-key but lucrative. The girls liked me because I made sure no harm came to them. They called me the Good Pimp. That was my reputation. I'd tell them that most men were all about wham-bam-thank-you-ma'am. I'd say, 'Honey, light a cigarette, lay it in the ashtray, and by the time it burns out, your customer should have had his satisfaction. Quick thrill for him, less work for you.' The gals would trust me with all their personal problems. I guess everyone needs a shoulder to lean on."

"The people running that Western Hills Inn ever get suspicious?"

"I gave the bellman a cut. Gave the taxi drivers a cut. Gave the maids a cut. Had everyone moving in the right direction. Word spread. Clean rooms, gorgeous gals. You wouldn't believe who came through. Big stars. Desi Arnaz."

"Lucy's Desi?"

"The same. Arrives in a limo. Throws around hundred-dollar bills like Monopoly money. Champagne for everyone. Party all night. Switch rooms. Switch girls. Two at a time, three at a time. Turns around, goes back to Hollywood, and a month later, he's back in Euless."

I shook my head in wonder. Paul got around.

★

Paul didn't find us any work that night in Dallas, but the evening proved lucrative in other ways. Paul always maintained his connections. The men we met we'd meet again. And, of course, he'd eventually find the man I was dying to meet most. Ray Charles.

Paul and I decided to take Fathead up on his offer to meet the High Priest of Soul. He gave us the address, and on Sunday afternoon, we headed back to Dallas. The thirty-two-mile drive on Highway 80 through Arlington was no sweat. Construction on a new turnpike was underway, and I liked looking at the heavy equipment—bulldozers, backhoes, track loaders, and rollers. I liked rolling down highways. Paul was a great companion because, like me, he'd rather listen to music than talk. The biggest song in the country was playing on the Buick radio: Tennessee Ernie Ford's "Sixteen Tons," followed by Ray Price's "Crazy Arms" and then Johnny Cash's "I Walk the Line." I was still noodling with songs of my own but hadn't had much success in getting them recorded by me or anyone else.

Ray's neighborhood was nice. Well-kept lawns, small houses. His was on Eugene Street. Fathead was at the front door to greet us. He introduced us to Ray's wife Della. A little toddler, Ray Jr., was chasing after the family puppy. The radio was tuned to KCNC, the Fort Worth country radio station where I'd been working. That was unexpected.

"Ray's out back," Della said, "working on his car."

Fathead led the way. There was the genius himself, hunched over the engine of a Studebaker Golden Hawk, a two-door hardtop coupe. He had on his dark glasses, a brown shirt, and brown pants. He didn't turn his head our way.

"Be with you fellas in a minute," he said. "Mechanic said he changed the spark plugs, but I can see that the spark plugs aren't the problem."

I was tickled by how he said, "I can see . . ."

We watched him dip in and out of his tool kit, fooling with the engine for a good fifteen minutes. He worked fast and looked like he knew what he was doing. He reminded me of a doctor doing surgery. Finally, he put down his tools and said, "I do believe the problem is solved."

Then he got in the car and turned over the engine. It purred like a kitten. Big grin on Ray's face as he threw the Hawk into reverse and backed it down the driveway without missing a beat. He walked up to the house—no cane, no seeing eye dog—and shook our hands as Fathead introduced us. Strong handshake.

"Car's not even a year old," he said, "and already acting up. Pisses me off, but you didn't come around to hear me bitching about my car. I hear you boys play chess."

"I'll sit out and let you musical geniuses play," Paul said.

"What's your instrument, Willie?"

"Guitar."

"Your friend's calling you a genius."

"He was really talking about you."

"Duke Ellington's a genius," Ray said. "Art Tatum's a genius. I'm good at what I do, but that's about it."

"Feel the same. A genius to me is Django Reinhardt."

"Him and Stéphane Grappelli. Man, that fiddle and guitar go so good together."

"I'll never be Django," I said.

"You don't need to be. We already got us a Django. Fats said that you're on the radio. What station?"

"You got it on right now. I didn't expect you to be a country music fan, Ray."

"Why not? Grew up on the Grand Ole Opry. Down in Tampa I was in a band called the Florida Playboys. Ever hear of them?"

"Can't say I have."

"No one has. We were mainly covering the hits of the day. Stuff like 'Kentucky Waltz.'"

"This was a Negro band?" I asked.

"Negro my ass," Ray shot back, slapping his thighs in delight. "I was the only pepper in the saltshaker."

"And no one gave you trouble?"

"Not if I played the right notes. Hell, I knew more country tunes than all those crackers put together. No offense meant."

"None taken," I said.

"Talking country music, I've never heard your radio show. When's it on?"

"Weekdays at noon."

"Usually not up by then."

"I wouldn't be if I didn't have to," I said.

"You like Hank Snow?" Ray asked.

"Who doesn't?"

"Thinking of recording his 'I'm Moving On.'"

"Be interested to hear how you'd do it."

With that, he walked over to the upright piano in the small living room. Next to the instrument was a table holding a stack of thick bound books.

As he sat on the piano bench, he asked, "You like reading, Willie?"

"I love it."

Ray pointed to the stack and said, "My braille books."

"Mind if I take a look?"

"Now I'm not believing you read braille."

"I don't. It's just that I've never seen a braille book before."

I opened the one on top and ran my fingers over the bumps. "Is this a sexy one?" I asked.

"Only if you think the Bible is sexy."

Paul laughed like he knew something no one else did.

"What else you reading, Ray?"

"I like Robert Louis Stevenson. I like *Treasure Island* and *Strange Case of Dr. Jekyll and Mr. Hyde*. I like Edgar Allan Poe's 'The Tell-Tale Heart.' I started reading all those books in school. They call it fiction. Then you got your nonfiction. Ever hear of Norman Vincent Peale?"

"*The Power of Positive Thinking*."

"You read it?"

"I try to do it," I said.

"Well, lemme try to do this Hank Snow thing."

He played it about the same tempo as Hank but with gospel flavor that turned it into a hymn. As a piano player, he made me think of my sister, Bobbie, who, like Ray, had come up in church where you learn chords big enough to get the whole congregation rocking. Ray's rendition got me rocking.

"Great," I said.

Ray got up from the piano and headed toward the couch. His movements were deliberate, decisive. His body and mind were on double time. It was invigorating to be in his presence.

"Ready to fool with these rooks and bishops?" he asked.

"Gonna give it my best."

"I'm just a beginner," Ray said.

"Sounds like a setup for a bet."

"You know what they say about robbing the blind," Ray reminded me. "I'm no gambling man. Are you?"

"Been known to put down a few dollars on dominoes."

"I like dominoes. Dominoes is fun, but chess is war."

"Go easy on me, Ray. I'm just a country boy."

"Backwoods Georgia, where I was raised, is so country we be eating everything on the hog 'cept the oink."

"Yeah, but you got a proper education. Look at that pile of books."

"State school for the blind. Saint Augustine, Florida. Learned me a little Beethoven."

"Wouldn't mind hearing a little Beethoven," I said.

"You keep pushing back our gunfight at the O.K. Corral."

"Come on, Ray," I said, "just a little Beethoven."

Ray went back to the piano and knocked off a little Moonlight Sonata.

"Mighty pretty," Paul said.

Determined, Ray brought out his board and set up the pieces.

"Right now there's still some daylight left," he said, "and you can see. That gives you one hell of an advantage. But come nighttime, we won't be turning on no lights. That's when your advantage ends and mine begins."

We chuckled, but when the sun set and it got too dark to see the pieces, I saw Ray wasn't kidding. He expected me to have memorized all the positions the way he had. So, of course he wiped me out.

"Tell your boss to push that radio show till evening time," Ray said on our way out. "I wanna hear what you sound like on the air. I wanna hear you tell the people how a blind man kicked your ass."

"Not sure how long that show's gonna last," I said. "If I keep playing those records of yours like I've been doing, they might wind up firing me."

Ray exploded in laughter. "You guys with your twenty-twenty better watch out for those wooden nickels," he said as we climbed in the Buick to head back to Cowtown.

★

That night Paul brought out his own chessboard.

"Watching you and Ray gave me the itch," he said. "You ready?"

"Never thought a guy with your background would be interested in chess."

"My background has everything to do with chess," he said.

"What part of your background?"

"Jail."

"They play chess in jail?"

"Killer chess. The killers are the best players."

I fought hard, but Paul's background bested me. He played to kill and won hands down.

It ain't no crime in a prisoner to steal the thing he needs to get away with, Tom said; it's his right.

MARK TWAIN,
The Adventures of Huckleberry Finn

HOUSTON

Coming Up on 1960

YOU WOULDN'T CALL IT a pretty city.

I'm sure it's got some pretty spots, but when I wound up there, nothing looked pretty to me. I was living just outside the city in Pasadena, close to a ship channel. I'd look out the window of my little apartment where I could see nothing but chemical plants polluting the air with waste. You could choke on the stink. The summertime season didn't help. Houston humidity can drive a sane man crazy. You never stop sweating.

All this would have been okay had I been making a living. But I wasn't. That was the only reason I'd left Fort Worth to come to Texas's biggest city. Yet I couldn't get a deejay gig. Couldn't find work in a club. One hope was to chase down Pappy Daily, who owned a record label that had me cut some tunes of my own back in Fort Worth, self-pitying songs like "No Place for Me." Pappy's label put out five hundred copies and sent me a bill. I tried hawking them on the radio, but damn few buyers bit. When I finally caught up with Pappy, he was all caught up with George Jones—his newest signing—and showed little interest in getting back in the Willie Nelson business.

"You got no future as a singer," he said, "but if you write something new, come back and see me."

"Lemme see what I can do."

There's an upside to the downside of despair. It can lead to creativity. Some called Houston "America's Industrial Frontier," others named it "The Planet's Petrochemical Center." Both descriptions would seem to poison the climate for decent writing, but, weirdly enough, I was able to turn my sorrow into song.

One song, "Family Bible," was about my spiritual upbringing. The other, "Night Life," was about not-so-spiritual hard times in Houston. I thought the tunes represented a good one-two punch: a ballad of faith and a story of the blues.

With new determination, I went back to see Pappy. Sang him the songs accompanying myself. I'm not much on self-congratulation, but I do have to say they sounded pretty smooth.

"I don't hear a hit," Pappy said.

"Does every song have to be a hit?" I asked.

"What else is this business about?"

I didn't bother to answer. We were from opposite worlds.

As it turned out, my mentor from Fort Worth, Paul Buskirk, had opened a guitar school in Houston. He heard the songs, bought 'em both for practically nothing, and got some guy named Claude Gray to sing 'em. Because Pappy liked Gray's voice more than mine, he put out a single of "Family Bible" that made some noise and started moving up the charts. That didn't mean money because Pappy didn't like paying anyone anything, but knowing my song was pleasing people did my spirit a world of good.

My simple philosophy is if you keep knocking on enough doors, someone's gonna let you in. That's how I wound up working at the Esquire Ballroom, a musty dusty joint out on Hempstead Road. As a sideman, I could pull in a few bucks. Though I was hardly qualified, Buskirk hired me as a part-time teacher at his guitar school, and a low-watt radio station hired me to work the five o'clock graveyard shift. Pay was peanuts. I was still struggling to make the rent for the small apartment where I was living with my wife Martha. Our family had quickly grown from one daughter—Lana—to another, Susie, and our son, Billie.

I couldn't hold on to the deejay spot, and the teaching thing dried up when I couldn't sign up any students. That meant the only steady income was my unsteady gig at the Esquire. I thought of packing it in. Back to selling encyclopedias or vacuum cleaners? How about driving a truck? How about driving the truck off a cliff? My mind was melting down. Being broke is bad—but being depressed is worse. Being both broke and depressed is pure hell.

The spell of hell was broken at the Esquire when, during a band break—even if the band wasn't paying me—I'd come out and, all by my lonesome, start singing some of these new songs I'd penned. Mostly the folks paid me no mind. They were there for fun, not to listen to some guy cry in his beer.

"Night Life" was a sad song. "Funny How Time Slips Away" was even sadder. "Crazy" was about a guy who gets dumped by a gal. "Mr. Record Man" was the story of another lonely soul living a lonely life. "The Party's Over" was self-explanatory. These songs were my repertoire. These songs were my heart. My heart wasn't exactly dancing at a time when the crowd wanted to do just that. Drink and dance.

"You've changed" was the first thing Paul English said to me when one night he turned up at the Esquire after I'd sung a set. I hadn't seen him for well over a year.

"You look good, buddy," I said. "You still in Fort Worth?"

"Moved to Dallas. Business was so good I expanded to Waco. Now I'm setting up shop in Houston."

"What kind of shop?"

"The kind frequented by men looking for love."

"Well, if you haven't changed, what makes you think I have?"

"Those songs. You write 'em?"

I nodded. Paul nodded back. Long silence.

"Want a beer?" he asked.

"Sure."

I knocked back a Lone Star.

"I think those songs are worth something."

"You're right. I sold most of them."

"For how much?"

"Enough to pay the rent."

"That don't sound smart," Paul said.

"Never claimed to be smart."

More silence. Another couple of Lone Stars. The band got onstage and started playing Hank Thompson's "I've Run Out of Tomorrows." They didn't sound too good.

"Aren't you in that band?" Paul asked.

"They already got a singer and a picker."

"Not nearly as good as you. You shouldn't be standing at the bar. You should be back onstage."

"You been playing drums, Paul, or does your other business take up all your time?"

"Oh, I'm playing. I got the music bug."

"You don't sound happy about it."

"The bug doesn't pay. But I love the bug. You gave me the bug."

"Well, you can give it back."

"It doesn't work that way."

"Where have you been playing?" I asked.

"Me and my cousin Arvel were with Ray Chaney's band at the Stagecoach Inn."

"The one in Fort Worth?"

"Over on the east side. Then I got hired by Good Time Charlie Taylor and His Famous Rock and Roll Cowboys."

"Good name."

"They gave me an even better name," Paul said. "Called me the Bip Bop Drummer. And they put me on a poster 'cause they said I look like Errol Flynn."

"You draw a crowd?"

"Nope. That's why I went back to my former profession."

"The pleasure profession."

"Pleasure always pays. Music doesn't."

"You'll get no arguments from me."

"But dammit, Willie, your music should be paying. You got something none of us got."

"I know you're not talking about money."

"I'm talking about talent," Paul said.

"Everyone's got talent."

"Not like you."

"Well, I do gotta admit that I needed a little cheering up. Thank you, buddy."

"Let's get outta here. There are better places to get cheered up."

"I'm ready."

I wasn't sure what Paul had in mind, but since I trusted him, I figured it wouldn't do me any harm and might get my mind off money—and the lack thereof.

Paul had a rooster-red Cadillac with a white top and fins that looked like jet engines. Red leather seats and a customized speaker system—the first I'd ever seen—that blasted music from all corners. We flew through the night. The Gulf Freeway. The Eastex Freeway. A blessed breeze had blown away the unpleasant smells of the city. Factory lights looked like crazy sculptures. Me and Paul weren't talking—we never had to—because we both knew that our BS couldn't compare with the soundtrack provided by the radio. Pushing the buttons, Paul switched from station to station. Roy Acuff. Jackie Wilson. Bill Monroe. The Platters. Bobby Darin. Buck Owens.

We pulled in front of a nondescript building that turned out to be Gold Star Studios. I knew about Gold Star. Every musician knew about Gold Star. Gold Star was where Lil' Son Jackson, a blues singer from Dallas, had cut his "Rockin' and Rollin'." Gold Star was also where Lightnin' Hopkins, who lived in Houston's Third Ward, did his famous "Tim Moore's Farm." The Big Bopper's "Chantilly Lace" was cut at Gold Star. So was George Jones's "Why Baby Why." Gold Star was big-time. It was the most sophisticated studio I'd ever seen.

Gold Star was owned by Bill Quinn. Bill Quinn knew Paul and said he'd heard of me.

"How?" I asked.

"Pappy Daily."

"Isn't that the guy who said he was gonna put out your records?" Paul asked me.

"Pappy Daily says a lot of things," Bill said.

"Willie is someone you gotta record," Paul insisted.

"Recording costs money," Bill explained.

Paul reached in his pocket and laid some cash on the soundboard.

"This should cover a couple of sessions," Paul said.

Bill said he'd call me to set up some dates.

That same evening Paul took me to a fancy nightclub where he introduced me to Don Robey, a light-skinned Black man who owned Duke and Peacock Records.

"Robey's the biggest promoter in the state," Paul said. "Mainly R & B acts, but his favorite color is not black. It's money green."

Robey was a talkative gent. Told us how he was the one who got Big Mama Thornton to sing "Hound Dog" and Gatemouth Brown to do "Okie Dokie Stomp."

"Good songs," I said.

"Wouldn't have happened without me. You got some good songs?"

Before I could answer, Paul answered for me. "We got songs like you've never heard in your life. Songs that will make your soul ache."

"What kind?" Robey wanted to know.

"He got him one song so blue you'd think Ray Charles wrote it himself."

"Sing it," Robey said.

"It's too loud in here," I said.

We went back in the alley, and, to the accompaniment of some screeching tomcats, I sang "Night Life."

"I like it," he said. "I'll call you."

He never did, but Bill Quinn came through. A couple of weeks later I went to Gold Star and cut a few sides.

Before that first Houston evening with Paul was over, we found ourselves at the Toddle House across from the ship canal. Another three o'clock breakfast. Hash browns and hot coffee. Looking out the window, I could see chemical plants a few miles off in the distance. They glowed a shade of dirty yellow.

When the night had begun, I was as low as I'd been for a long while. Then Paul came along. Paul had the ability to make anyone feel like a winner.

"Hang in" was all Paul had to say. "Something good's gonna turn up for you here."

At that moment the Toddle House rocked from an explosion. I looked out the window and saw that one of those plants was up in smoke. A few minutes later, sirens were screaming and ambulances racing down the road. Everyone was rattled. Everyone except Paul.

"Them chemical plants remind me of the chemicals I use to put in my hair," Paul said as he started on his third cup of coffee. Coffee always got Paul talking. "We called ourselves the Peroxide Boys. It was me, Lunkhead, some kid named Cowboy, and another called Lamebrain. We were two-bit hijackers. We'd bust up pinball machines. We'd hold up some stuffed shirt walking out of a bank. Once we got busted four times in the same day. We always found a way out and a way back. The guys we wanted to be—Cecil Green, Tincy Eggleston, Benny Binion—these were the old-timers who showed us what it meant to enforce. Take Herbert Noble, Benny's number one competitor. Benny hated him. Benny did his level best to eliminate him. But Herbert's nickname wasn't 'The Cat' for nothing. They said he had nine lives 'cause that's how many times he gave Benny's boys the slip. Until one morning when he strolled down his lawn, opened his mailbox, and got blown to bits by the bomb inside. That's why that explosion back there didn't bother me. I'm used to explosions. Hell, when I was coming through the ranks, there were more bombings than baseball games. I remember one week when three different fellas from three different gangs got bumped off in three different ways—knife through the heart, shotgun to the head, noose to the neck. For some reason, though, bombings became the go-to method. You didn't have to be there when it happened."

"I'll be careful next time I go for the mail."

Paul laughed. "You're the last guy in the world anyone would want to harm. And if they did, well . . ."

Paul didn't finish his sentence. Maybe because the Toddle House cook had turned on his transistor radio, and Marty Robbins was singing "El Paso," a Texas story that Texans like me and Paul had to hear.

By the time Paul dropped me off at the shoddy apartment complex where I was living with my family, black night had turned grayish blue.

"How long are you in Houston for?" I asked him before saying goodbye.

"Who knows?" Paul answered. "How about you?"

"Who knows?"

"Since I don't know when I'll see you again, Willie, you better take this."

He handed me a wad of cash.

"What's this for?"

"Buying back those songs you sold, you stupid son of a bitch."

★

I got into Gold Studios, where I did some work that turned out halfway decent, mainly because Paul Buskirk was in charge. I was still too green to understand how to put together a record. Buskirk wanted me—and not Claude Gray—to sing "Night Life." I was glad to sing it, but when the single came out, it said, "Paul Buskirk and His Little Men featuring Hugh Nelson." Hugh's my middle name. Never understood why it got billed that way, but what the hell. Buskirk issued it under a label he created called Rx. Felt like a prescription for disaster. It pretty much was. None of the recording work I did in Houston left an impression on anyone. Well, I take that back. One guy was impressed.

★

Paul English was on the phone.

"You still in Houston?" I asked.

"Long gone."

"Where you calling from?"

"Laredo."

"What are you doing there?"

"You don't wanna know. What are you still doing in Houston, Willie?"

"Stuck."

"Well, get unstuck. I ran into a record promoter down in Mexico. Uncle Hank Craig. Says he knows you."

"What's that old horse trader up to?"

"No good, as usual. Selling holy water on his radio stations along with baby chickens and genuine autographed pictures of Jesus."

"I always liked that guy."

"He likes you. He's been playing your 'Night Life' down here. Friend of mine also heard it up in Cleburne. You seen any money yet?"

I laughed.

"Well, Willie, all I can say is that the record's great except for the drummer. He's not following you right."

"Tried to tell him, but he said my timing was off."

"The hell with him. How long are you gonna stay stuck in Houston?"

"Till I build up my courage."

"To do what?"

"Remember me telling you about how I met Mae Axton?"

"I know the lady well. She worked for Colonel Parker and sent me an autographed picture of her and Elvis and a gold-colored copy of 'Heartbreak Hotel.'"

"Well," I said, "when I met Mae she was promoting Hank Snow. Anyway, I played her my 'Family Bible' song. She listened and then said three words I keep hearing in my sleep."

"'Get a job?'"

"Nope. The lady said, 'Get to Nashville.'"

"Sounds 'bout right, Willie. All the big-time songwriters work out of Nashville."

"I hardly see myself as big-time. That's the problem, Paul."

"That's your problem and no one else's. If you're not big-time, then Jayne Mansfield doesn't have big tits. Big-time is nothing but an attitude."

"It's something I need to think about."

"No, it's not. It's something you need to do. Willie, get your ass outta Houston before Houston eats your ass up."

Paul and Willie in a hotel room on tour somewhere across America.

Martin and Lewis were a great comedy team—and they were both good musicians—but they didn't last. They fell out. Willie and Paul are probably a better comedy team and better musicians—and they have lasted, and hell will freeze over before they ever fall out.

ROGER MILLER

NASHVILLE

Early '60s

"KING OF THE ROAD," the famous Roger Miller song, said, "Trailers for sale or rent." Well, we rented ours at the very place Roger was singing about: Dunn's Trailer Court. Used car lot on one side, cemetery on the other. I made it to Nashville, but from where I was sitting, the city wasn't exactly pretty.

This was me in my late twenties, trying to get a handle on things. I couldn't. I'd been encouraged by pals like Paul and pros like Mae Axton to make my mark in a city where country music had made many an artist a millionaire. But after months of hustling, I was still a pauper. This trailer park was several levels below the way my family had been living. Our run-down apartment in the boondocks of Houston looked better than the view of the tombstones right outside our dilapidated home on wheels.

My get-up-and-go attitude was challenged. That's saying something because my get-up-and-go attitude is deep inside my DNA. It's always been there, and I had believed, at least till I got to Nashville, it always would be. But Nashville was different. I hadn't ever lived in a place where singers and songwriters formed a big, vibrant community. I wasn't unwelcome in that community. But my problem was seeing how so many of its members were making a living making music while I wasn't. Not a dime. Not only was no one interested in my songs, I had a hell of a time finding a barroom where I could sing. I had to go back to hawking encyclopedias. And because my heart wasn't in it, I failed at that.

The one thing I *could* do was drink. But I was hardly what you'd call a good drinker. I'd either get sullen or, even worse, get crazy and pick a fight with someone twice my size. I'm not a bad fighter, but, if you do fight, it's best to stay well within your weight class.

Tootsie's Orchid Lounge was the spot. That's because it was two steps from the Ryman Auditorium where the Grand Ole Opry performed. You'd see everyone at Tootsie's, all the stars and would-be stars. As a would-be, I saw it as "water, water every where, nor any drop to drink."[3] Here's Jim Reeves. There's Buck Owens. Say hello to Hank Locklin. Meet Ferlin Husky. These were all good guys who were writing good songs, looking for good songs, and recording good songs. Somehow, though, my songs didn't seem up to snuff.

Looking back over my life, my early days in Nashville were a definite low point. I'm not one to easily fall prey to depression, but depression had me in its grips. Throwing back bourbon on a freezing cold night at Tootsie's, I thought about an old song I'd heard Lightnin' Hopkins cut back at Gold Studios in Houston. He sang about feeling so bad until he lay his head on some lonesome railroad line and let it ease his troubled mind. So why not?

It had started snowing. There wasn't any railroad in sight, but there was Broadway—the city's main thoroughfare. Why not go out there, lie down in the middle of the street, and let some souped-up Plymouth Barracuda ease my troubled mind?

So I did. I lay, prepared to stay. Eyes closed. Ready to move on and move out. If this world wasn't working, maybe the next one would. I lay for five minutes, then ten, then fifteen. Don't know why—maybe it was the bad weather and the late hour—but there was hardly any traffic. If one or two drivers saw me, they swerved out of the way. Was I relieved? Was I disappointed? Can't say for sure. All I know is that I got up, went back to Tootsie's, and had another drink.

★

"How in God's name you find me here?"

"I'm keeping track of you, son. You gotta know that by now."

Paul English was leaning on the hood of our trailer. It was four in the afternoon, and I was barely awake. It was the day after I'd tried to ease my troubled mind on Broadway. Paul's timing was uncanny.

Last night's storm had passed and left a bright blue sky in its wake. As usual, Paul was looking sharp. Clean as a whistle. Happy as a lark.

"A sight for sore eyes," I said.

"What you got to be sore about?"

"Rough night."

"Nice day."

"Didn't know you had clients in Nashville," I said to Paul.

"Got clients everywhere. Was up in Louisville and figured I'd stop by on my way to Memphis to see how you're doing."

"As well as could be expected," I said.

"I got high expectations."

"I got an empty stomach."

"Well then, enough said." His smile was wry and devilish and sweet. You never knew what was going to come out of his mouth next. "I got a lady who runs a rib joint down by Music Row that'll put the pep right back in your step, brother."

The rib joint was called Juicy Lucy's. Lucy lived up to her name. Green-eyed beauty with a personality as sweet as her peach cobbler. She ran the little place herself, running back and forth from the tiny kitchen to waitress the four tables where her customers lavished her barbecue with praise. Like Paul, her family came from Vernon, Texas. They said they were kissing cousins, but I'm guessing they were more than that. Paul introduced me as the hottest songwriter to hit Nashville since Hank Williams.

"Who happens to be cold as ice," I said.

"They say when Hank Williams came to Nashville, the Grand Ole Opry wanted nothing to do with him," Lucy said. "Making a name for yourself in this town takes time."

"I was just about to tell Willie the same thing," Paul said. "But coming from you, the words go down a little smoother."

Lucy smiled in a life-is-worthwhile way that lifted my heart. The pork ribs, potato salad, and cobbler lifted it even higher.

After lunch, Paul and I took a walk down Music Row. All the majors had offices and studios. Acuff-Rose. RCA. Columbia.

"We gotta go out tonight and celebrate," Paul said.

"Celebrate what?"

"You being here."

"I may not be here too much longer," I said.

"Why do you say that?"

"Look at these names on these buildings, Paul."

"Biggest names in the business."

"And not a one is letting me through the door."

"That's even more reason to celebrate."

"You're not thinking straight."

"I'm thinking of how these fools are gonna feel when you start having hit songs left and right. That's when they'll eat their hearts out for paying you no mind when they could have bought you for a nickel and nail."

"So, we're celebrating the far-off future, is that it?" I asked.

"Isn't far off at all. The past was Juicy Lucy's and her red-hot ribs. The future is now. Boy, don't you know that we're always living in the future?"

That evening I lost track of the future. I lost track of everything. Me and Paul went barhopping. Before long, I was wasted on whiskey when some brute started bad-mouthing Texas. Turned out he was an Okie. To borrow Merle Haggard's famous phrase, he was an Okie from Muskogee. I actually like Muskogee. I've played there. The Arkansas River runs right by. My people come from Arkansas. I once won good money playing dominoes in Tulsa. All us southwestern folks have a world in common. But this big ole boy was insulting Texas farm boys. As a certified member of the Future Farmers of America—I'd joined back in Abbott as a preteen—I took exception. I also took a swing. And missed. The Okie I missed wasn't about to miss me. He was about to crown me with a bottle of Pabst Blue Ribbon when Paul caught his arm and convinced him otherwise. On to the next bar.

The next day I woke up at noon. The hangover was monumental. Paul was on his way to Memphis. I took the kids to the park while Martha worked her afternoon shift as a waitress at the Hitching Post. At the time, she was carrying our family's finances. That fact hardly helped my mood. But Paul's trip had helped. In spite of my acting the fool at the bar the previous night, it was good being with someone who seemed to believe in me more than I believed in myself. He really believed in a rosy future at a time when I couldn't afford to buy my wife a dozen roses.

I wasn't sure about rosy thinking. Maybe that's because I had no concrete plans for hustling my music other than hanging out with the music hustlers whose hustles were working. That meant showing back up at Tootsie's to scope out the scene I'd already scoped out more times than I cared to remember. It was the same ole shit.

Except this time it wasn't. Something had changed. I'm not saying it was Paul's quick visit; Paul really had nothing to do with it. Paul didn't even know Hank Cochran. Along with Mel Tillis, Hank was one of the first guys I met when I arrived in Nashville. More than the others, Hank had shown an interest in my writing. On this particular day his interest took a different turn. He made me an offer. Said he'd been hired by a publisher who paid him to write songs and thought maybe he could get me hired as well. It was an actual job that he worked, more or less nine-to-five. The idea floored me. Someone might be willing to pay me to sit around and write?

"Think so," Hank said. "But the pay isn't great."

"Not looking for great. Just looking to be a professional songwriter."

"Well, look no further."

The publisher was called Pamper. Interesting name cause I did feel pampered. Never before had I been given an empty office and told to do nothing but write. I greeted the walls with "Hello Walls," a song Faron Young recorded. The thing ran up to number one, and the next I knew, Ray Price decided to give my "Night Life" new life and, even better, hire me as a bass player in his band, the Cherokee Cowboys. Ray didn't even care that I didn't know how to play bass.

Paul had predicted my immediate future, and when I saw him next, down in Texarkana, he had another prediction. The Cowboys had shared the bill with Patsy Cline, who'd recorded "Crazy," one of those forgotten songs I'd written down in Houston that turned into her biggest hit. All to my surprise.

"You're hotter than a pistol," Paul said after the show. "I just don't see why you don't have your own band."

"I've always dreamed of being a Cherokee Cowboy," I said. "Ray knew Hank Williams. Lived with Hank Williams. Took over Hank's band when Hank died. Ray Price is a link to a history I started dreaming about when I was a kid. Besides, he's a great guy."

"I'm seeing the link between you and the gal he's got singing with you."

"Shirley Collie?" I asked.

"The yodeler."

"She really gets me."

"That's what I'm saying, Willie."

"We have a tight harmony."

"How tight is tight?"

I didn't have to answer Paul because he already knew the answer.

Later that year—1962—I divorced Martha (or, to be more precise, Martha kicked me out), and in 1963 I married Shirley.

Shirley and I left Ray Price and formed our own group. I also cut my first album. It was for Liberty Records, who still saw me more as a writer than a singer. That's why they titled my debut album, . . . *And Then I Wrote*. Critics said my singing was out of kilter cause my time was out of kilter. Critics don't buy records, but in this case neither did the public. The album, featuring a clean-cut Willie Nelson on the cover wearing a conservative suit and tie, flopped like a flounder out of water.

I cared, and I didn't care. I cared because no one likes failure. But I also didn't care because I liked my style of singing—I couldn't imagine singing any other way—and had no intention of changing. The singers I admired most—everyone from Louis Armstrong to Jack Teagarden to Ernest Tubb to Jimmie Rodgers to Crosby and Sinatra—had quirky styles. Those styles sounded natural. They sounded conversational. When I sang, I was looking to have a musical conversation. No more, no less. If you didn't like the conversation, fine. If you did, so much the better.

The release of this first album, despite its meager sales, did wonders for beating back the blues. It brought out that hustler energy. When I'd arrived in Nashville two years earlier, that energy had been exhausted. I felt revitalized by a new marriage and a new career.

On April 29, 1963, I turned thirty. Song royalties were slow to accrue, but there was definitely money coming in. And even though my album didn't earn me a cent, I was able to tour. I even got a gig at the Golden Nugget in Vegas. It was a kick to ride down the Strip and see the marquees advertising Liberace and Wayne Newton. At a time when the Rat Pack was riding high, the town still had room for a country act like mine.

After Vegas, I was back in Dallas. It was an especially happy occasion because I was playing the Longhorn Ballroom, now owned by Dewey Groom. That's where I'd seen Hank Snow and secretly dreamed that maybe one day I could play the place. That one day arrived. And so had Paul English.

"Drove up from Galveston just to see you," he said. "I had to be here for this."

"Glad you came, Paul."

"You'll be even gladder when I tell you what I've arranged."

"What's that?"

"The Willie Nelson Ballroom, a place that'll make the Longhorn look like a tearoom. It's a million-dollar operation."

"And who's underwriting this million-dollar operation?" I asked.

"Jack Ruby."

It is one of the blessings of old friends that you can afford to be stupid with them.

RALPH WALDO EMERSON,
Emerson in His Journals

DALLAS

1963

GOD BLESS PAUL ENGLISH. God bless Paul for many reasons. First, his devotion. Second, his guts. Third, his vision. He could see the future. Unfortunately, his vision wasn't perfect. It was fueled by optimism, a quality you gotta love. Being an optimist myself, I went along with Paul's program, even though, I now admit, his program was outlandish.

Paul explained the whole thing to me over lunch at the Dallas Petroleum Club in the Baker Hotel downtown. He said to be sure and wear a suit. That was a good tip because this was the fanciest lunchroom in Texas. The chandeliers looked like they came from Buckingham Palace. So did the red-upholstered chairs. Mahogany and marble were everywhere you looked.

"If you look over there," Paul said, "that's Lamar Hunt sipping Chivas Regal with Clint Murchison Jr. Between the two of them, they control half the oil in the state."

A few years back, Murchison had brought his Dallas Cowboys into the NFL, and Hunt had recently brought the Dallas

Texans into the AFL before turning them into the Chiefs and moving them to Kansas City.

"How the hell did you get into a place like this?" I asked.

"Like everyone else. I walked through the front door."

"Come on, Paul."

"I got the hostess her job here. Carol's a former employee of mine destined to go places."

"Oh, Paul, it's you," our waitress said. She was a six-foot blond dressed in a tailored black uniform.

"Hey, Goldie," Paul said. "Carol hire you?"

"She did."

"Good things are happening to all the girls." Paul nodded contentedly.

"The steaks here are great," Goldie assured us.

"Give us the best two."

"You know I will, Paul. Who's your friend?"

"Willie Nelson."

"I've heard of Willie Nelson," Goldie said. "You're playing the Longhorn this week, aren't you?"

"I am."

"Well, I'm going to try to get over to see you."

"Please do."

"See that, Willie," Paul said after Goldie was gone, "you can hardly go anywhere without being recognized. That's why Jack Ruby is ready to do for you what O. L. Nelms did for Bob Wills."

"What's that?"

"Build the biggest venue in Dallas–Fort Worth and name it after you. He wants to call it Willie Nelson's Music Hall."

"And put it where?"

"Arlington. Halfway between Dallas and Fort Worth."

"I once had an apartment in Arlington," I said. "Arlington's a wasteland."

"Willie, look at the man sitting at the table next to Murchison and Hunt. Know who he is?"

"No."

"Angus Wynne Jr. He built the Six Flags Over Texas amusement park right in Arlington. It's a big hit drawing big crowds. Dallas from the east. Fort Worth from the west."

"I don't want to be fenced in by having to play one venue."

"You won't be," Paul explained. "Bob Wills didn't have to play his Ranch House but four weeks a year. It'll be the same for you."

"I thought you said Ruby was a gangster."

"Hell, Willie, most promoters are gangsters. The music business is gangster paradise."

"What's Ruby willing to give me for using my name?"

"Ten percent of the gate for every show. Thirty percent for your shows."

"You trust him?"

"Of course not."

"Then why are we dealing with him?"

The steaks arrived along with baked potatoes. Goldie was right. The meat was sweet.

"Here's what's happening with Ruby," Paul said. "He bought an interest in the Bob Wills Ranch House from Nelms. Then he lost it. Then he got the Singapore, the Silver Spur, and Hernando's before buying the Sovereign Club. He turned the Sovereign into the Carousel to compete with the Weinstein boys. Trouble is, the Weinsteins are untouchable. Brother Barney makes a fortune with his Theater Lounge, while brother Abe is raking it with his Colony Club."

"You took me there," I reminded Paul.

"The Colony Club is still the top-drawer strip joint in town. Ruby's Carousel never developed the right clientele. See the guys having lunch in this Petroleum Club? They're the right clientele. They're spending their money with the Weinsteins. That's why Ruby's looking to go in a different direction. He sees Arlington as your kingdom. He thinks you could be the king of Arlington."

"Do I want to be the king of Arlington?"

"No, you want to be the king of Texas, but Arlington could be the way to get there."

"And how's that gonna happen? I'm living in Nashville, Paul."

"Nashville's never gonna love you like Texas loves you."

"Nashville loves hits. As long as I write hits . . ."

"You'll never stop writing hits. Hits are not the point. The point is that you're a singer as much as a writer, and more than anything, you're a performer. I can see that's what makes you happiest."

Paul wasn't wrong. But Ruby wasn't right. Through Paul, I learned later that Ruby supposedly bought some land in Arlington, just off Highway 80, and hired a contractor. But before construction could begin, the contractor ditched the project because Ruby hadn't come through with the money. Ruby's moneymen in Chicago were having legal problems. His backers backed out. That's when Ruby went to friends in Vegas, sold his vision, and got new underwriters. The contractor said he was ready to break ground the minute the underwriters' check arrived. The check arrived on a Tuesday and bounced on a Wednesday.

Not about to give up, Ruby hired a whole new team of financiers from El Paso. Paul called them unsavory characters, but since unsavory characters never scared off Paul, Paul hung in. He said he'd keep careful tabs on what was going on. Not to worry.

★

On November 22, 1963, I was headed to Dallas to meet with Paul, who said these characters, along with Ruby, wanted to meet me. Before sealing the deal, they needed my personal assurance that I'd perform opening night.

I was at the Nashville airport, about to board the plane, when the news came in. President Kennedy had been shot and rushed to Parkland Hospital. During the flight, the captain said the president had been pronounced dead. When I landed at Love Field, Paul was there to greet me. He was as shook up as me.

"Dallas will never be the same," he said. "Right now, things here are crazy. I have a feeling, Willie, we better stay away from Ruby. I'm not sure he's anyone I want to get you mixed up with."

That was a big about-face, but I didn't argue. Paul always had my best interests at heart.

Two days later on live national television, Jack Ruby, wearing a fancy fedora, emerged from a crowd of reporters and, point blank, shot Lee Harvey Oswald to death.

★

Some years passed before, rather than Paul making a proposal to me, I made one to him.

"Hey, Paul," I said, "how'd you like to live on pig farm?"

"Who owns a pig farm?" he asked.

"Me."

"Then count me in."

Paul in the late '70s doing his thing,
in the early days of playing with Willie.

I guess Nashville was the roughest
But I know I've said the same about them all
We received our education
In the cities of the nation, me and Paul

"ME AND PAUL"

THE KENTUCKY/ TENNESSEE BORDER

1967

PAUL MOVED TO THE RURAL compound I'd bought in Ridgetop, thirty miles outside Nashville. Unlike me, Paul wasn't a farm boy. It wasn't easy for him to leave the big city.

Before the move, he'd been in Houston where he ran his various businesses. My own music business had, as usual, its ups and downs. Songwriting royalties were good, but record sales weren't. Liberty dropped me, and, even though RCA picked me up, RCA had the same problem as Liberty. They didn't know how to produce or market my music. The head man, Chet Atkins, was a genius guitarist and producer. I loved Chet, but Chet tried putting me in a box that couldn't contain me. This was the era of big studio productions with a producer—not the artist—in charge. I went along because this was how Nashville worked. I was a cog in a music machine.

"You still sound good," Paul told me when my band turned up in Houston for a gig. "You even sound better in my car. Lemme show you what I mean."

Paul had taken my first RCA album, *Country Willie: His Own Songs*, and transferred it to a tape cartridge he played on a four-track machine customized for his new Lincoln Continental. I'd never seen a setup like that before.

"The record is great," Paul said, "but I still see them selling your songs more than they're selling you."

"They're trying to sell us both together."

"Is it working?"

"Do you mean have they sent me any big checks?"

"That's just what I mean."

"No big checks. I also need drummer."

"Wasn't Johnny Bush doing the drumming?" Paul asked.

"He was also doing our books. But Johnny's more a singer than a drummer. No one's got a voice like Johnny. I want him out front singing. So, I'm looking for Tommy Roznosky. You got his number?"

"Tommy's the wrong drummer for you."

"What makes you say that?"

"Because I'm the right drummer."

Paul's words gave me pause. The thought hadn't occurred to me. I say that not because Paul wasn't a good drummer but because Paul was running his own operations that brought in big cash. Playing drums behind me would mean a considerable financial bringdown.

"I don't pay good," I said plainly.

"I don't need good," Paul said even more plainly. "But I do have one earnest question."

"What is the question?" I asked.

"Do you want me as your drummer?"

"I'd be a damn fool not to. When I'm up there singing, who else is dumb enough to stay out of my way?"

"You flatter me."

"I tell you the truth. Now do you want to know the salary?"

"No. Don't need to hear anything that might make me change my mind."

★

A week later, Paul was on board. Our first gig was in San Diego. Posters had been advertising "Willie Nelson and His Record Men," the name of my group at the time.

"Not a good name," Paul said.

"Why?"

"Because the boys in your band are not making the records with you. You said Chet Atkins is in charge of the records and putting in his own musicians."

"The name will have to do until something better comes along. Meanwhile, you're gonna have to learn the songs we're playing tonight."

"Already know them."

"How's that?" I asked.

"I've been to a thousand Willie Nelson shows and listened to Willie Nelson records a thousand times. What else do I need to know?"

"Nothing, I guess."

I guessed right.

Drummers are strange creatures. I respect them. They got those tubs they like beating on. They have those cymbals they like crashing. They got those snares they like snapping. Of all the instruments, the drums might be the most fun. They bring out the little boy in the big man—and that's a good thing. Music needs to be fun. Take it too seriously and you go nuts. Like Little Richard said, rip it up.

But drumming is one thing; drumming behind a singer is another, especially when it comes to a singer as offbeat as me. Some singers need a drummer to kick their ass. I understand that. Some singers need a boost. But I wasn't built that way. When I'm singing, I'm basically telling a story. And because my storytelling style can wander far off the road before it winds its way back, I need a drummer who's willing to wander off with me. Paul English was that drummer.

Before that night in San Diego, it had been years since we'd played together. Yet nothing had changed. Paul drummed with me the way he talked with me. He gave me lots of space. He also loved using the brushes. Paul was more a brush man than a stick man. Sticks are fine, and sometimes you need that kind of snappy syncopation. But brushes allow more nuance. Brushes are quieter. Paul became a master of the brushes.

Another thing that made Paul different from other drummers: he wasn't scared of silence. My singing style is heavy on pauses. It's as much about what I don't sing as it is about what I do sing. During those small silences, Paul knew just how to lay out or, with great restraint, lay in. He understood that I'm not a fancy talker, and I'm not a fancy singer. But in both talking and singing, I do have a flavor that can easily be overwhelmed. That flavor is subtle, and Paul got it even better than I did. He knew how to preserve that flavor. So rather than kick up, Paul kicked back. Rather than bring attention to himself, Paul got out of the way and let me have my say. He played less when he could have played more. He played under when he could have played over. He played just right.

All those songs about going crazy in the night life and letting time slip away, songs about talking to walls and wrapping up Christmas presents with pretty paper, songs about record men getting drunk when the party's over or families getting religion reading the Bible—Paul knew to accent them with a perfect combination of flair and care.

I'm guessing that the year of our reunion was 1967. If I'm right, from that night on Paul would be my drummer—and ever-steady friend—for the next fifty-three years. Uninterrupted. Undisturbed by discord. Unbothered by a single harsh word. And, in my case, too often unconscious from the overconsumption of booze.

Liquor changed my disposition. I could get mean and violent. That's really not my nature. That should have been obvious to me. Someone could have pointed that out. That someone could have been my best friend Paul. But what made Paul my best friend was his knowledge of me. He knew when I was receptive to a new idea and when I wasn't. Giving up drinking was a new idea that, at least for a while, I just wasn't willing to consider. Paul was a big part of the reason I finally changed my mind.

★

Let me back up to that first night in San Diego. After the gig, Paul and Johnny Bush crossed the border into Tijuana. Normally, I would have gone along, but I was too tired to party.

I'd known Johnny since we were both Cherokee Cowboys in Ray Price's band. I believed in Johnny's talent. He wasn't called the Country Caruso for nothing. Plus, he could write. Yet for all his musical talent, Johnny struggled with life on the road. Raised a hard-shell Baptist, he suffered from guilt whenever he did something the church might not condone.

"It was a wild night," Paul told me the next afternoon. "I wound up taking Johnny to the hospital."

"What happened?"

"He was throwing up blood, but the doctors say he'll be all right. He's got an inflamed stomach."

"He still in the hospital?" I asked.

"They'll be discharging him in a few hours."

"I'll go with you to pick him up."

Johnny was waiting for us in the hospital lobby. He looked pale as a ghost.

"God was punishing me," he immediately said.

"Well, the punishment is over because the doc said you're fine," Paul assured him.

"Only reason I wasn't punished more is because you were sober, Paul, and got me help."

"I just did what anyone would do," Paul said.

"Willie," Johnny said, "I gotta give up this stuff."

"We all do," I said.

"I think I've been taking on too much. Paul's helping me out by drumming so I only have to worry about singing. But I've also had to worry about doing your books, arranging the payroll, and dealing with the promoters. I'm feeling too much pressure."

"Don't worry about it, Johnny," I said. "Paul can handle all that."

Paul just nodded. And from then on, that's the way it was. There never has been a better bookkeeper or a better handler of promoters than Paul.

I saw that in handling Johnny—with all his complicated feelings about drinking and living wild—Paul could handle anyone. He could handle the whole band. In my whirlwind of a life, Paul was the strongest force around me. Because he had both feet solidly planted on the ground, he made sure I didn't get swept up and carried off by windstorms coming my way.

Without my asking or telling him, he knew the benefits I derived from being around him. For example, when that California tour was over, Paul accompanied me back to Ridgetop and eventually, along with his beloved first wife Carlene, moved to a house on the farm. Carlene was beautiful in all ways.

She met Paul back in 1958 when Paul was playing and doing the bookkeeping at Ray Chaney's Stagecoach Inn in Fort Worth. Charlie Owens, a steel guitarist, was also in the band. Two young women—Carlene and her best friend, Loretta—from Glen Rose, a little town fifty miles away, came to the big city to do a little partying. Paul fell head over heels in love with Carlene, and Charlie fell for Loretta. Carlene had a young son, Darrell Wayne. Long story short: Paul married Carlene, and Charlie married Loretta. From that moment on, Paul treated Darrell Wayne as his own. He became a caring father. In Ridgetop, Carlene and Darrell Wayne became an intimate part of our family.

Paul and I were aiming for the same thing—domestic happiness. Paul managed that a lot better than I did. In my case, the challenges were many. By then both my mom and dad, divorced since I was a baby, were living in different parts of the farm with their spouses and stepchildren. I'd also invited my grandmother, Mama Nelson; my sister, Bobbie; and her three sons. Even my first wife, Martha, was there with her third husband—along with our kids, Lana, Susie, and Billie—while me and Shirley, my second wife, were living together while already having the kinds of problems I'm prone to have with beautiful and talented women.

★

Pigs are damn smart animals. I'm crazy about pigs. I was excited about the possibility of making a little money as a hog raiser. Johnny Bush, who was also up at the farm, felt the same. Like me, he'd grown up in the country and seemed to know what he was doing.

"Neither of you know what you're doing," clear-eyed Paul said.

No matter. We built a pen and bought a bunch of weaner pigs. Problem was, Johnny and I did the construction work ourselves and made the lower plank too high. Next thing we knew, pigs were escaping like convicts out of Sing Sing. It was a shit show, but we finally rounded them up and pushed them back in the pen. Problem solved. Except it wasn't. Because we put the water trough right next to the feeder, the pigs had no reason to roam. Later I learned that the feeder needs be far from the trough so the pigs have to keep moving. If not, they'll get so fat they can rupture—which is just what happened. Bottom line: the operation crashed.

On the morning that Johnny and I sold off the remaining pigs for a fraction of what I'd paid, he and I were out there pulling the pen down. Paul happened to walk by. The great thing about Paul is that he not only didn't say, "I told you so," he didn't even look over at us. He just kept walking.

★

When it came time to ride into Nashville to cut a new record, Paul usually accompanied me. He made the trip because he was my biggest booster and got a kick out of watching me record. And also because he knew my habit of heading to the barroom after the session was over. That's where I was prone to provoke someone who didn't need provoking.

I've always been a funny fighter. My natural inclination is to move away from violence. At the same time, I grew up loving competitive sports and was halfway good at most of them. As time went on, I embraced martial arts and earned my fifth degree at tae kwon do. In my midthirties, I earned my tenth degree in barroom brawling. I never considered myself a drunk—and still don't. It's just that whiskey turned me stupid. Paul knew that and wasn't about to let me go off and be stupid without him. It's stupid to get your brain bashed in when your brain isn't even working. On booze, my brain went underwater. Paul would not let me drown.

During the recording sessions themselves, you'd think Paul would have had an attitude. After all, he was the drummer in my band, but producer Chet Atkins didn't use him on the record. Most musicians would take offense. Paul never did. He understood what I was doing. I was deferring to the powers that be in the hopes that Nashville could turn me into more than a hit songwriter. The idea was to turn me into a star.

One session had to be particularly painful for Paul. Chet knew I had a big following in Texas and decided to have me record *Texas in My Soul*. Three of the songs—"Waltz Across Texas," "There's a Little Bit of Everything in Texas" and the title cut—were written by Ernest Tubb, the Texas Troubadour. Paul was as Texas as a Fort Worth slaughterhouse. He loved Ernest Tubb as much as I did. He knew Tubb's music as well as I did. And he also knew he could damn well provide me the right rhythm to sing those songs. But when Chet put the band together, he had another idea. He wanted Johnny Bush on drums.

"Why?" I asked.

"Paul's fine," Chet answered, "but Johnny's more polished."

"Is polish what we're going for?"

"We're going for hits, Willie, and we need to get the studio sound exactly right."

Paul was standing close enough to hear this discussion. As I kept on questioning Chet, Paul took me aside.

"Let the man have his way, Willie. If he doesn't produce the record he wants, RCA won't promote it. RCA has the muscle to make it a hit."

Paul was right, and he was also wrong. Chet produced it his way, RCA promoted it, but it was hardly a hit. Back to the drawing board.

★

Back on the road, Houston remained one of my favorite spots. That's because I'd met a Houstonian, a young lady named Connie Koepke, who for a number of years had been my girlfriend. Paul knew about Connie because Paul knew everything about me. But Paul wasn't about to say a word. That's how I wanted it. Life on the farm with Shirley was one thing. Life on the road was another. Hopefully, the twain would never meet. Unfortunately, they did. Connie got pregnant by me and had a baby. We named her Paula Carlene after Paul and his wonderful wife Carlene. Shirley discovered what had happened when she opened a Houston hospital bill detailing the birth of my new daughter. Shirley went wild. She was inconsolable.

Paul had his own way of consoling me.

"Look," he told me, "you wanted this marriage to end or you wouldn't have had the bill sent to Ridgetop."

"I didn't tell them to send the bill," I said.

"Connie gave them her address, but you intentionally told them to send the bill to you in Tennessee."

"Well, I couldn't let Connie pay, could I?"

"Of course not. But you could have had the bill sent to me, or to your office, or to anywhere but to your home."

"You're saying that, subconsciously, I did it on purpose?"

"That's just what I'm saying," Paul said.

"You're also saying you know me better than I know myself?"

Paul didn't have to reply. His smile said it all.

★

Domestic stability didn't come naturally to me. It took me until middle age to really settle down. At thirty-six, I still had a long way to go. In 1969, Shirley moved out of Ridgetop, and Connie, along with baby Paula, moved in. My dream of one big happy family didn't last long when my daughter Lana came over to my house with her face bruised and her nose bloody.

"What happened, baby?" I asked.

"Steve."

Steve was Lana's husband.

Without a second's thought, I jumped into my pickup, found Steve, and slapped him so hard he fell to the ground. I left him there. Before going back home, just to make my point, I took my .45 and shot out the left front tire of the pride of his life, his Pontiac Firebird. I thought that'd be the end of the story. But it was just the beginning.

Steve had a bunch of brothers with a bunch of guns. The whole crew came roaring over to my house, ready to do battle. That's when Paul took over. Paul was ready. He brought out his M1 rifle with .380 bullets and blasted the bumper of the Firebird. That frightened them off so bad that the next day, hat in hand, Steve showed up to apologize.

I didn't have anything to say, but Paul did.

"I shot your bumper just to scare you," he said. "But if you hadn't driven away in a hot hurry, I would have blown your sorry butt to bits."

On a package show in Buffalo
With us and Kitty Wells and Charley Pride
The show was long and we're just sittin' there
And we'd come to play and not just for the ride

Well we drank a lot of whiskey
So I don't know if we went on that night at all
But I don't think they even missed us
I guess Buffalo ain't geared for me and Paul

"ME AND PAUL"

BACK IN NASHVILLE

Late '60s

"KARMA IS A BITCH." That's a quote attributed to Kris Kristofferson. I met him in the 1960s in Nashville. I liked him from the get-go. Before he was a janitor at one of the studios, he'd been an army helicopter pilot and a Rhodes Scholar. I'd done some reading in metaphysics and knew the concept of karma—what goes around comes around—but Kris put it in a new light. Karma could bite you in the ass.

I saw that happen on one of my endless road tours. I'd just finished recording another one of those RCA albums that wound up collecting dust on record store shelves. This was after Bob Dylan had come to Nashville and all the producers wanted to give country music a folk flavor. I didn't mind. I'd always thought my music was for folks anyway. I sang Kris Kristofferson's "Once More with Feeling" and Joni Mitchell's "Both Sides, Now"—beautiful songs. Just to be perverse, I also did a new version of something I'd written a few years earlier, "I Gotta Get Drunk."

"You're drinking too much," Paul kept telling me. Paul was the only one who could or would talk to me that way. Not that my band members were afraid of me. I don't think anyone's ever been afraid of me. But others figured I wouldn't listen to them. Paul figured otherwise—and he was right, although it took me too long to heed his advice.

★

Buffalo should have been the turning point. Buffalo was freezing. Buffalo was snowbound. Buffalo was the North Pole of country music shows. Our bus—a 1947 Flxible Flyer on its last legs—slipped and slid over the icy road and barely made it to the venue. I can't remember everyone on the bill that night, but it was one of those packaged supershows. I remember Kitty Wells. And I was glad to run into Charley Pride. When Charley first got into the business, I met him in Dallas where Dewey Groom wouldn't let him sing at the Longhorn Ballroom because Charley was Black. Once again, Paul came to the rescue. He ushered in Charley through the stage door. When I got onstage, I introduced Charley. Paul kept a vigilant watch over the crowd. No one was going to hurt Charley. And because Paul had a strong arm on Dewey's shoulder, Dewey wasn't going to make a move. Charley came to the mic, and before he sang a note, just to make a point, I kissed him on the lips. When Dewey heard Charley singing "The Snakes Crawl at Night," he became a believer. Afterward, the two of them got silly drunk at an all-night guitar jam—which we called a pulling session—and wound up passed out on the same bed.

Well, there I was in Buffalo getting silly drunk myself. Blame it on the weather. Blame it on the long wait before going onstage. Blame it on a head cold I felt coming on. The blame game could go on forever. The simple fact is that I got so drunk I couldn't even remember performing.

★

Miami was as hot as Buffalo was cold. After the show in Miami, I wasn't as wasted as I'd been in Buffalo, but I was half-looped. That's why I did what I normally never did. I ventured into Paul's territory. That happened after the show, when the promoter said he was willing to pay only half of what he'd promised.

"It's all or nothing," I said, taking over Paul's role.

Paul came into the office in the middle of the negotiations.

"Let's the two of us discuss this outside, Willie," he said to me.

I agreed.

"My pistol is in the bus," Paul said. "I'll grab it and come back. The negotiations will be over before they start. You stay here."

But when Paul tried to get back in, the doors were locked. We wound up with nothing.

Wasn't but a few weeks later when we were playing New Orleans that Paul got a call from a friend in Miami. The promoter who'd stiffed us had been blown to bits.

I kept remembering Kris's words: "Karma is a bitch."

Paul swore he had nothing to do with it.

★

Phoenix, Arizona. Great music town. Special place for me because it's where I first heard Waylon Jennings at JD's, a club out by Arizona State. Waylon and I became brothers. JD's was a huge venue. Can't recall the name of the barroom where we were playing on this particular visit, but it was a third the size of JD's. It was another night where I'd had a drink too many. It was also another time when the promoter wasn't willing to pay what he'd promised. But I had learned my lesson and let Paul handle it.

Paul came to the bus with a deep frown.

"You didn't get the money?" I asked.

"Don't worry. I will."

Tired as all hell, I fell asleep. When I woke up, I looked out the window to see a Thunderbird being raised to the sky by a giant forklift. The forklift drove off with the T-Bird. A few minutes later, the promoter came running out, screaming at the top of his lungs.

"Where are they taking my car?"

"Pay up and I'll let you know," Paul said.

The promoter paid up.

When it came to getting paid, Paul would not be denied. His experience in repossessing cars, one of his early jobs in Fort Worth, came in handy.

"You go in with two things," he explained. "An attitude and a gun. Those two things guarantee that you'll come out with the money."

His protective attitude went beyond me. Poolrooms are notorious for mischief. During this same Phoenix trip, Paul was at a poolroom with my stepbrother Doyle, who'd just won a bet beating two guys. Neither was willing to pay. Paul wouldn't have it. He wouldn't even discuss it. He coldcocked the first guy while the second started choking him with a pool stick. That didn't stop Paul from grabbing his own pistol from the back of his belt and shoving it up his assailant's left nostril. Doyle's winnings were immediately paid in full.

★

Paul wasn't a drinker, which was probably why he helped me see how drinking was doing me damage. If we had been drinking buddies, it might have been a different story. But booze didn't bind us. Brotherhood did.

After a show in Texarkana, a fan slipped me a joint. I had tried pot before. Fred Lockwood, a musician who worked the down-and-out clubs with me on Jacksboro Highway in Fort Worth, was the first to ask me to "blow some tea."

I didn't know what he meant.

"Weed," he said. "Grass. Take a hit. You'll feel good."

I didn't feel much of anything.

When I was a Cherokee Cowboy, pot was also in the air. Tried it again. Still no buzz.

But on this drizzly night in Texarkana, something changed. Probably the quality of the pot. After I took a few tokes, I glanced toward the back of bus where Paul was doing some bookkeeping.

"How's it looking?" I asked.

"Good," he said. "We got a percentage of the gate, and the gate was good. How's that pot?"

"Mellow," I said.

Mellow wasn't a word I usually used, but it seemed exactly the right word to describe my state of mind. I felt my mind slightly altered. The alteration was subtle but satisfying. I had a feeling of reassurance. It wasn't that everything was going to be all right. Everything *was* all right. Right now. I listened to the rain hit against the windows. The rain had a rhythm I'd never noticed before. The rain represented replenishment. I thought back to those droughts that we'd lived through when I was a kid in Abbott. When rain finally came, we celebrated. "That's God weeping with joy," Mama Nelson always explained.

I watched the raindrops wiggle their way down the windows. The formations were fascinating. I saw them as liquid sculptures. I loved how they were close yet separated and remembered words I'd recently read by Kahlil Gibran in *The Prophet*: "Let there be spaces in your togetherness, and let the winds of the heavens dance between you." The raindrops were doing a dance. "Love one another," Gibran had written, "but make not a bond of love."[4] As these words went through my mind, our guitarist, Jody Payne, got on the bus, took out his guitar, and began to strum. The sweetness of his chords brought Gibran back to mind. "Even as the strings of a lute are alone," he wrote, "they quiver with the same music."[5] Quivering raindrops. Quivering notes. A sense of well-being. A sense of divine order.

"The books are in order," Paul said, coming from the back to sit next to me. He had studied the books of Gibran more closely than I had.

"Looks like that grass put you in a good place," he said.

I knew what else he was going to say, so he didn't have to say it. I read his mind telling me, "Weed beats the hell outta booze. Put down that moonshine. It's slippery, and it sneaks up on you. Poison for your heart and your bones."

And I did.

★

Me and Paul and the rest of the band never stopped working. We did so not just because we loved being on the road but also because we had to. The RCA superstar plan hadn't exactly worked out, and I couldn't live on song royalties. Live gigs were our bread and butter. They were also how we maintained a loyal fan base. Since my records were on the slow-to-no rotation on radio stations, performances were mandatory. How else would folks get to hear me? Connecting with fans—then and now—is everything. If some fans yell out, "We love you!" my way of giving that love back has always been to sing them a song.

My other way of staying alive creatively was writing songs. Though I'd finally seen that whiskey was not my friend, I nonetheless wrote a whiskey song. I did it because I've never wanted to be preachy. I wasn't about to decry the sins of drinking. A song is a song, not a sermon. "Bloody Mary Morning" remains one of my favorites because I believe it's a good story. Like all my songs, it's my story while, at the same time, not my story. It could be my story. It could be yours. It could be anyone's. It's the story of a guy who wakes up in L.A. with a hangover. While he was passed out, his gal left him. Realizing she's gone, he knows he's got to get out. So, he boards a plane for Houston. Drinks a Bloody Mary. Thinks over his life, a country boy confused by the pitfalls and deceits of the City of Angels. Can't even remember why Houston is his destination. Doesn't matter. Nothing matters cause it's a Bloody Mary morning.

That big booze song became part of our repertory. I also started singing "Whiskey River" around the same time I stopped drinking whiskey. I didn't write the song—Johnny Bush did—but I loved the metaphor. I loved singing about how Whiskey River needed to take my mind and block out the tortuous memories of the loves I'd lost. I'd been there and done that.

I took my cues from writers like Edgar Cayce, who taught about the power of the mind to connect to the Infinite.

Positivity is everything. I didn't want to be *against* anything. It was enough to be *for* something. I was for marijuana because I saw the plant as beneficial. As the years went by, I studied the plant—in addition to smoking it—and learned that those benefits were far greater than I'd ever anticipated. I became an advocate and remain so to this day.

★

Me and Paul were off the road for the holidays. Hank Cochran came to Ridgetop to write with me. In one day we turned out no less than seven songs. That has never happened to me before or since. Ridgetop was a great place to write, but could I see myself living there forever?

The question was answered December 23, 1970. Paul thought it'd be fun to go into Nashville to see the fellas at Lucky Moeller's annual holiday party at the King of the Road, a club named after Roger Miller's great song. Roger might have even been there. I was pleasantly high on the local reefer. Paul was telling back-in-the-day stories, when Fort Worth made Dodge City look like Disneyland.

In the middle of the party, I got a call from Bobbie's son Randy. He was hysterical. He had every right to be. He said my house was on fire. Thank God no one was inside. The family got out in time.

"Ask him about the garage," Paul prompted. "See if it's caught fire yet."

It hadn't.

"Good," Paul said. "Tell Randy to pull your old car in there. So, when it burns, insurance will get you a new one."

We left the party and rushed back to Ridgetop. Flames everywhere, but the house was still standing.

"There are two things we gotta get out of there," Paul said.

I knew what he was talking about. Two guitar cases—one with my beloved guitar, Trigger, and another that held two pounds of primo pot.

"I'll get those cases for you," Paul said.

But by then I had already made a dash inside and was able to retrieve the valuable goods.

Back outside, I stood there watching. Naturally, there were tears. Naturally, there were fears. I tried to comfort everyone. Our house was gone, but our spirits were not.

That night, Connie, Paula, and I stayed with Paul and Carlene. The next morning, Paul and I went to survey the damage. It was a total loss.

"Looks to me like it's time to go home," Paul said.

By "home," Paul meant Texas.

As that thought came to mind, so did the name of the seventh song I'd written with Hank Cochran the day before: "What Can You Do to Me Now?"

BACK TO TEXAS

1970

IT ISN'T THAT PAUL DIDN'T like Nashville. He adjusted to life both in the city and country. Up on Ridgetop, he even got to like the pigs. But he saw what had been obvious to me for some time. The Nelsons and Nashville weren't the right fit.

"You can't squeeze a round peg into a square hole," Paul told me, "and you are no square."

After the fire, Paul and I had the same notion at the same time. We belonged in Texas because we were Texans. We were bred in Texas, and, during these long years when my records weren't selling, it was those big ole venues in Texas—the Cotton Club in Lubbock, Big G's in Round Rock, and the Longhorn in Dallas—that kept us alive. Our Texas fans were the most loyal.

Paul pointed out that the highlight of my ten-year Nashville tenure—an invitation to join the Grand Ole Opry—wound up costing me money because, to do the broadcast, we couldn't leave the city on weekends. The broadcast pay was paltry. I could have made ten times more on the road.

Nashville was the center of the country music world, but that world, at least for me, burned up along with my house. I needed out. That's when Paul, in his minimalist manner, said three magical words.

"Call Crash Stewart."

Crash Stewart had been booking my band in Texas for years. He was one of the promoters who kept us going. He was also one of the promoters Paul didn't have to muscle for money. Crash loved us.

"Crash knows the state better than anyone," Paul said. "He knows we've got a traveling circus, and he'll find a place to put us."

That place turned out to be a dude ranch—Lost Valley—an hour outside San Antone. The place was big enough to house my ever-growing tribe of family and friends. Because it was January, the ranch was shut down, and the owners were willing to rent it out. Even in wintertime, Texas gave me that warm vibe I'd missed in Tennessee.

Lost Valley Ranch in the little town of Bandera wasn't anything you'd see featured in *Architectural Digest*. It did have one thing, though, that made a difference: a golf course. The PGA had hardly sanctioned it, but Paul and Bee Spears, my longtime bass player, started playing right away. Before Lost Valley, I'd never given much thought to golf. I liked contact sports—football and basketball, boxing and martial arts. I'd tell Paul, "What's the point of chasing a tiny white ball over a pasture of weeds?" The Lost Valley golf course was rough and rocky.

"Don't knock it till you try it," Paul said. "I have a feeling you're going to like it."

More than like it, I loved it. I got addicted. It's easier to explain an addiction to women than an addiction to golf.

Romance is easier to understand. Sex is certainly easier to understand. The more you get, the more you want. But why should hitting a ball with a club captivate you until you find yourself playing the game for the rest of your natural life?

That first day in Lost Valley, I got lost in the experience. Paul, Bee, and I played twenty-four holes. Then another twenty-four. Then it started to rain.

"I've had it," Paul said.

"Just one more round," I said.

"It's pouring."

"We won't drown. The rain just makes it more challenging."

"Golf is making you crazy," Paul declared.

"Craz*ier*," I corrected him.

★

Winter, spring, summer, and fall. Traveling from Lost Valley to Longview, from Little Rock to Memphis, back down to Baton Rouge and over to Galveston. Then right back to Bandera where I could chase that little white ball until the sun went down.

Being away from Nashville had me thinking differently. The idea had always been to write and record a hit. The music biz is built on hits. But albums like the Beatles' *Sgt. Pepper's Lonely Hearts Club Band* didn't follow that formula. The Beatles found an overall concept to give coherence to a string of songs. Almost like a suite.

Could I do that? Should I do it? What was the point in doing that?

"You should do whatever you wanna do," Paul was always saying. "Artists got free license."

So, I used my free license. I gave it free range. Wrote a record I called *Yesterday's Wine*. Wrote about God. Wrote about romance. Wrote about what it'd be like to go to my own funeral. Even wrote about the adventures of hanging out with Paul, putting the final touches on the song that gave this book its title:

Almost busted in Laredo
But for reasons that I'd rather not disclose
But if you're stayin' in a motel there and leave
Just don't leave nothin' in your clothes

And at the airport in Milwaukee
They refused to let us board the plane at all
They said we looked suspicious
But I believe they like to pick on me and Paul

I wrote this suite of songs with an open heart and an open spirit. Felt great about it. Turned it in to RCA to see how they felt.

"It feels soft," one of the label bosses said.

I asked him to be more specific.

"The hippies have been getting in your head," he said. "This stuff is too far-out for country music fans. You'll lose your audience, Willie. You gotta rein yourself in and do what you've always done."

Do what I've always done?

What *had* I always done?

"It's not real complicated," Paul said after I told him about RCA's negative reaction to the record. "You've always done what feels right."

"The record company guy said I need a plan," I said.

"You're not a planner. You're a doer."

"Except I'm not sure I know exactly what I'm doing."

"You never have," said Paul. "You kinda let the wind control you. That's what makes you, you. That's what makes you so special."

★

Bob Hope . . .

. . . Bing Crosby, Frank Sinatra, Nat King Cole, Jerry Lewis, Dean Martin, Spencer Tracy, George Burns, Cary Grant, Gregory Peck, Sidney Poitier, Jimmy Stewart, John Wayne . . .

The autographed photos of all these celebrities hung in the window of Sy Devore's men's clothing store in Hollywood. Paul spotted the store before me. That made sense because Paul had always been more interested in his appearance than I was in mine.

During the '60s, I didn't think much about style. The covers of my albums featured me as your average guy in a turtleneck and a sport coat. Nothing fancy, formal, or stylish.

Paul always had style, and, as styles were changing in this new Age of Aquarius, he, like most everyone, was reevaluating his wardrobe.

"Let's take a look inside," he said.

Why not? Who doesn't appreciate a pair of fine Italian loafers? An English sport coat of pure cashmere? Shirts of the softest Egyptian cotton? Silk ties from Charvet?

"Beautiful stuff," I said, "but none of it is right for you."

Paul agreed, and just as we were walking out something caught my eye: a jet-black velvet cape with a silk bloodred lining.

"Try it on," I urged.

Paul did.

"What do you think?" he asked.

"Makes you look like Satan himself."

"Perfect. I'll take it."

He took out his wallet, but I beat him to the punch. I put the cash in the salesman's hands.

"What are you doing, Willie?" he asked.

"No one else is going to get credit for dressing the devil. This is all my doing."

"Just remember, though," Paul added, "the devil's the prettiest angel in heaven."

Paul had a whole cape collection, all black, all red-lined, all designed to maintain the image he cherished most. He augmented the image by growing his sideburns a little longer and maintaining a sharp-edged goatee. His black hat, black shirt, and black slacks added to the ominous look. Some people saw it as frightening. I saw it as funny. Women loved it. Paul became a star and dressed like one.

Playing Panther Hall in Fort Worth was always a homecoming for Paul. Never will forget the first time Paul presented himself to old friends, enemies, and neighbors in his new devilish guise. He not only wore the outfit like he was the proud Prince of Darkness himself but also laid dry ice around his drum set so smoke would rise up off the floor. Satan surrounded by smoke. Fans loved it. Paul was an instant hit.

When it came to my own image, the changing times allowed me to hearken back to olden times. Olden times basically meant T-shirts and jeans. That's what I grew up wearing. My takeaway from the hippie era was basically, "Do not concern yourself too much with society. Wear what you want. Do what you want. Be who you want to be." What I wanted was comfort. It was comfortable not to think about clothes, so I didn't. It was comfortable to let my hair grow long, so I did.

It was comfortable to slip on a headband so my forehead wouldn't sweat, so I started wearing headbands. I dropped the pretense. Dropped the nonsense. Stopped trying to look one way or another. Just reached for the first thing in the drawer—a souvenir sweatshirt from my pal Zeke Varnon's joint in Hillsboro and a pair of old overalls—and got going.

I had no problem if others wanted to stage their appearances. Take Leon Russell. Leon was my bridge to a new generation of fans. He was one of the greatest entertainers. Great pianist, writer, and singer. Nine years younger than me, he kept his country roots and combined them with rock and soul. He became a cultural avatar. His "Mad Dogs and Englishmen" tour with Joe Cocker set the world on fire. Leon was avant-garde. Like Paul, he got himself a costume. Sometimes it was a white top hat and all-white suit. Sometimes it was a custom-made cowboy hat with sparkles and fringes and green lizard boots.

When it came to boots, Paul had Leon beat. To mirror the red lining of his cape, he wore red snakeskin boots custom-crafted by a friend.

"Who's the friend?" I asked.

"Buddy I met in jail back in the fifties. I got out and never went back. He kept going back until they wouldn't let him out at all. But he did learn a craft. Best boot maker in Texas. When he heard that I was sporting this new get-up, he decided to do it one better. Best present of my life. Who's gonna outshine me now?"

If you had to guess, you might say Little Richard. Richard was the original cape man. They said he had a walk-in closet stuffed with nothing but capes. Well, I guess the cape-off was inevitable. I'm just glad I was there to witness it. Happened in Nashville.

Little Richard was living in the presidential suite of the Hilton across from the Country Music Hall of Fame. We were in town for a gig and happened to be staying at the Hilton. That first evening we left our rooms and were waiting at the elevator bank. Doors opened. Out stepped Little Richard. The man looked absolutely regal. We'd met before. He graciously greeted me, "Hello, Willie." But his eyes didn't stay on me. His eyes focused on Paul, who was in full costume.

"My, my, my," Richard said to Paul, "your cape is twice as long as mine. Mine stops at the waist. Yours practically kisses the floor."

"But yours has rhinestones and beads," Paul said. "And besides, I'm just a drummer. You're Little Richard."

Bless Paul's heart. He knew just what to say. Little Richard beamed, waved to us like he was the king of England, and went on his way.

★

While we're on the subject of the art of personal possessions, I want to point out another one of Paul's talents. He was a brilliant leather tooler. Earlier in his life, he had worked for the Fort Worth Tandy Leather firm making saddles. Like a magician, he could take a rough piece of leather and work the stylus, swivel knife, and camouflage tool. My *Tougher Than Leather* album features Paul's handiwork. On either side of my face, he designed a symmetrical vine of flowers and made the whole thing pretty as a picture.

In the name of candor, let me also point out that Paul had a predilection for decorative porn. Only Paul would apply that predilection to a .45 pistol. His favorite gun had a twin-sided image. The right side of the barrel showed a man enjoying intimate favors from several women at once. On the left side the guy returned the favors. He was depicted delighting some lucky lady. On the front of the barrel—the section of the gun you'd see as someone was about to blow off your head—were the words, *Welcome to Hell.*

Paul with his favorite set of Rogers drums. He was an ambassador for them and appeared on the cover of Modern Drummer *playing this set.*

If you're asking, "Who's crazier—Willie or Paul?" the answer is simple: Who the hell knows?

MERLE HAGGARD

ARRIVING IN AUSTIN

Early '70s

AUSTIN TURNED OUT TO BE heaven—at least for me. But it took me a while to understand it was the best place to launch whatever musical mischief I might be planning. My first notion was to move from the Lost Valley Ranch to Houston. After New York, L.A., and Chicago, Houston was, after all, the fourth biggest city in the country. Connie was pregnant with Amy, our second daughter, and I knew she'd like raising our children in her hometown.

I also figured Paul would like the idea. He knew Houston like the back of his hand. He could finagle us onto the greens of exclusive golf clubs while making sure we played all the big-time venues.

First time the topic came up with Paul was when we were driving from Nashville to Texas and stopped for lunch at a little place in the hills of Arkansas. My grandparents, Mama and Daddy Nelson, grew up in the Ozarks before settling on more fertile land in Abbott. My mother's roots were also in deep in Arkansas soil. On that day in 1972, I was thinking about my distant past even as I was considering my immediate future. I'd just put down a deposit on an apartment in Houston.

"Big mistake," Paul said while we awaited the arrival of our barbecue pork sandwiches.

I took a swig of my sweet iced tea before asking why he felt that way.

"Look where you are in your career."

"You know better than anyone where I am. I just recorded what'll probably be my last record for RCA."

My recent Nashville session was for an album called *The Willie Way*. I liked it. It featured almost all new songs I'd written. The big exception—the tune I'd wanted to sing the first time I heard it—was Kris Kristofferson's "Help Me Make It Through the Night."

"You don't think RCA will pick up your contract?" Paul asked.

"Not if the thing doesn't sell. And I have no reason to believe it'll sell any more than the other stuff I cut for the label."

"So why move to Houston?"

Before I answered, the waitress arrived with our sandwiches. I took a big bite. The pork was succulent and the sauce tangy.

"I don't know, Paul," I answered honestly. "Seems like the right place for a new start."

"Been thinking about one of those songs you just recorded. The one about your future."

"'Wonderful Future,' I called it."

"That's the one. You remember the last two lines?"

"'Scenes from the past keep returning, I've got a wonderful future behind me.'"

"Great lines. But what do you think they mean?"

"You know better than to ask me what my songs mean, Paul. I just write 'em."

"And I just listen to 'em. But what I'm understanding is that you just saw the future. The future really is just behind you. The future just happened."

"Where?"

"Dripping Springs."

A month or two before, a huge three-day music festival took place in Dripping Springs on a ranch west of Austin. Some folks were comparing it to Woodstock. The first night featured old-school artists like Earl Scruggs. The second featured Roy Acuff and Hank Snow. We came on the third night with Waylon, Kris, and Merle.

"How many people do you think were out there?" Paul asked.

"Ten thousand. Maybe more."

"And where you do you think most of them came from?"

"All over. But I'm guessing the majority from Austin."

"I'm guessing the same," Paul said. "Were you surprised to see so many hippies?"

"I was happy to see them. Happy to see everyone getting along."

"That's Austin. It's the one place in Texas where that's possible. That's why I see Texas as the future. Your future. Just like you and Nashville were never a natural fit, you and Austin fit together like a gun in a holster. Austin gets you."

"What's to get?" I asked.

"The Willie Way."

I laughed. "That's just a title I came up with because I couldn't think of anything else."

"All I'm saying is that the Willie Way was going in one direction, and now it's moving in another. It's moving to where Willie doesn't have to worry about anything except being Willie."

"And Houston's gonna get in my way?" I asked.

"Houston loves oil and gas and chemicals. Houston loves real estate. Houston is not going to love you like Austin loves you."

When Paul started talking about a city actually loving me, another line came to mind from Kahlil Gibran: "When love beckons to you, follow."[6]

I had no doubt that, during these changing times, I felt more loved in Austin than anywhere. A lot had to do with my sister, Bobbie. She had moved there and was playing piano at supper clubs. As kids, we'd started out together in the same band. That was over twenty years ago. I'd always dreamed of us being in the same band again. Maybe that could happen in Austin. Maybe Paul was right. Maybe Gibran was right. Maybe you don't follow your head. Maybe you follow your heart.

★

One thing I was right about: *The Willie Way* didn't sell like hotcakes. It didn't even sell like cold cakes. RCA said goodbye, but I wasn't bitter. I gave RCA credit for trying to get me over. I also wasn't bitter about Nashville. Nashville helped me make it as a songwriter. If Nashville couldn't turn me into a celebrity, it didn't deserve the blame. I didn't know then—and don't know now—who and what makes a celebrity. All I knew was that I was being prompted by two of the most important people in my life—my pal Paul and my sister, Bobbie—to pitch my tent in Austin.

The tent was a small apartment on Riverside Drive. Out our front window we had a view of Town Lake. Late one afternoon Paul came over and said he was taking me out to West Lake Hills to meet a musician he knew.

"He's crazy," Paul said. "Even crazier than you. Ever hear of the Sir Douglas Quintet?"

"Not sure."

"They had a hit few years back. 'She's About a Mover.'"

"I remember. Catchy tune."

"Well, Sir Douglas is a made-up name to sound English. Sir Douglas is actually Doug Sahm, a San Antone boy I saw playing around Alamo City years ago. He was trying to cash in on the English invasion. Now he's here and got a near-permanent gig at a place called the Soap Creek Saloon. I was up there and told him I'd bring you. He's your biggest fan."

"Sir Douglas?"

"He dropped that name and is back to being Doug."

Doug turned out to be a genius. A generation younger than me, he knew all the music of my generation. Seemed like he knew the music of every generation. He could play the hell out of any style. We bonded like brothers.

He introduced me to the longhair crowd in glowing terms. Then he asked, "Will you do a duet with me on one of your songs?"

"Which one?"

"'Me and Paul.'"

Paul was grinning from ear to ear. No wonder he'd wanted me to meet Doug.

"I'm going to New York," Doug said, "to a do a record with Atlantic. Their big producer Jerry Wexler got me the deal. And the first song I'm singing is 'Me and Paul.' Guess who's playing harmonica on it?"

"Got no idea."

"Bob Dylan. He heard the song and said, 'Yeah, that's the one.'"

I didn't know anyone besides Doug who could get Dylan to work as a sideman.

"I also got Fathead Newman to play sax on the album," Doug added.

"We know Fathead from Dallas," Paul said.

"He told me."

Doug's record turned out great. I liked his version of "Me and Paul." I also liked bringing my own band to the Soap Creek Saloon. Because it was a hippie hangout, I especially appreciated the warm reception. The crowd was just as eager to hear me play old stuff like "San Antonio Rose" as newer stuff like "Fire and Rain."

Soap Creek set us up for the next big move we made in Austin: the Armadillo World Headquarters. The 'Dillo was to Austin what the Fillmore was to San Fran. The Grateful Dead. Captain Beefheart and His Magic Band. Frank Zappa. Commander Cody and His Lost Planet Airmen. Hot Tuna. Quicksilver Messenger Service. They all played at the 'Dillo.

But would my style of music—however you labeled it—go over in this huge venue where the Flying Burrito Brothers ruled the roost?

"Hell yes," Paul assured me.

"These groups are all gussied up in crazy outfits," I said. "We just go out there in T-shirts and jeans."

"Speak for yourself, Willie," Paul said.

Paul was right. At least we had the black-caped devil on drums.

For months, it felt like we owned Soap Creek. The crowds kept getting bigger. By the time we played the 'Dillo, I'd lost all doubts about getting over to this new crowd. The so-called generation gap didn't exist. When Waylon showed up, he still had his hard-core West Texas cowboy attitude. He wasn't sure Austin was his spot. Paul reassured Waylon, and Paul was right. Waylon did great at the 'Dillo. Same kids who were loving Led Zeppelin were loving Waylon.

It was paradise.

SOMEWHERE IN TEXAS

WAYLON JENNINGS AND PAUL ENGLISH were crazy about each other.

Waylon saw Paul for what he was: a brilliant guy who could solve complex word puzzles with his left hand while doing the books for my band with his right hand. Waylon also liked that Paul was a true fellow Texan who was willing—even eager—to put his life on the line for friends. Without ever saying it, Waylon might have wished Paul was working for him instead of me.

Consider these two concepts: competition and brotherhood. Often, they are both at play. Take me, for example. I was an athlete as a kid. Played all the sports. As an adult, I got into golf and martial arts. Always loved dominoes and poker. Games are about winning, and, same as everyone else, I like to win. As a songwriter, money isn't my main motive. I write to express myself, but I'll be damned if I'm not thrilled to see my song hit the top of the charts.

As an artist, I've been blessed to bond with brother artists. Ray Price was my brother. Roger Miller. Ferlin Husky. Faron Young. Merle Haggard. Kris Kristofferson. Johnny Cash. Charley Pride. Ray Charles. Mel Tillis. Hank Cochran. Harlan Howard. And, of course, Waylon. Yet although the brotherhood was strong, there was always an undercurrent of competition. That's just being human. I never fell out with any of these fellas. I loved them. But I was aware of their successes, and they were aware of mine. We rooted for one another even as we rooted for ourselves.

Case in point: Waylon's "Bob Wills Is Still the King." It came out at a time when Austin had really embraced me. I loved what Waylon wrote. Loved it because it was a tribute to my idol Bob Wills. Even more, I agreed with the sentiment. There's no replacing Bob Wills as the King of Western Swing. But Paul took exception to the song. He made his feeling known when, in '75, Waylon came to sing at the 'Dillo.

Paul and I were there. I got a kick out of hearing Waylon sing about how, like me, he grew up in Texas honky-tonks, how we loved hearing Tommy Duncan sing with Wills, how he got hooked on western swing; I didn't even mind when Waylon sang, "It don't matter who's in Austin, Bob Wills is still the king."

After the show, we were hanging out in Waylon's dressing room when Paul said, "Look, Waylon, it does matter who's in Austin. Willie's in Austin. Right now, Willie's king of Austin."

"You're taking the song too seriously, Paul," I said.

"It's a serious song," Waylon corrected me. "It's a tribute song, and I don't intend to change a word."

"You shouldn't," I agreed.

"You shouldn't take a shot at Willie," Paul said accusingly.

"I even mention Willie in the song. I say that Austin is 'the home of Willie Nelson, the home of western swing; he'll be the first tell you, Bob Wills is still the king.'"

"That's right," I said.

"That's wrong," Paul said. "Willie might say that, but most of the fans have forgotten who Bob Wills is. Or never even knew."

"That's why I wrote the song," Waylon said.

"I don't like the way it makes Willie look. Like he's trying to be something he's not."

"Willie's the greatest," Waylon said. "Everyone loves Willie. Austin is his town. All I'm saying is that we best not forget history."

"I still say you're a little jealous," Paul said.

"How jealous can I be?" Waylon asked, "when I sing *your* song."

"What song?"

"'Me and Paul.'"

"Willie wrote that song," Paul said, "not me."

"But it's a song about you, and I love singing it," Waylon said.

"That's something else I want to mention to you, Waylon," Paul said.

"Mention what?" Waylon asked.

"You mess up the song," Paul said.

"He does?" I asked. "I don't hear Waylon messing up anything."

"You sing the wrong words," Paul said. "You don't sing 'me and Paul.' You sing 'me and Tompall.'"

"That's because I'm talking about Tompall Glaser. You know Tompall and his brothers?"

"Sure, I know 'em," Paul said.

"Great singers," I said. "Tompall had the first independent studio in Nashville. Nineteenth Avenue South. Hillbilly Central."

Waylon said, "Me and Tompall are about to release what they call a compilation album. I'll be singing some of my songs, Jessi will be singing some of her songs"—Jessi Colter was Waylon's wife—"Tompall will be singing some of his songs, and, if you agree, Willie, you'll be singing some of yours."

"Which ones?" I asked.

"Well, sir, the first is going to be 'Me and Paul.'"

"With the original lyrics?" Paul asked.

"Naturally," Waylon said. "Willie wouldn't sing anything except the original lyrics."

"Then why don't *you* sing the original lyrics?" Paul asked.

"Cause Tompall is to me what you are to Willie," Waylon said. "He's my best friend. We been through thick and thin together. When I sing the song, I just want to be true to myself."

"Better to be true to the right lyrics," Paul said.

"Waylon's got a point," I said. "Truth be told, I'm flattered he's singing the song at all."

Paul still wasn't placated, but I sure as hell was when that album came out. It was called *Wanted! The Outlaws* and became the first country album to sell over a million copies. And depending on your outlook, it also blessed or saddled us with the label of "outlaw" country singers.

Paul had his own feelings about that.

Next time we saw Waylon was in Brentwood, a hillside suburb outside of Nashville. Jessi called their place Southern Comfort. It was a beautiful home surrounded by lush gardens.

"Is this where the big bad outlaw lives?" Paul asked.

Waylon ignored his sarcasm and gave Paul a hug. He knew Paul looked up to him—just as Waylon looked up to Paul. He also knew Paul liked giving him a hard time.

Neither Waylon nor I could really argue with this outlaw business. It was making us money. Some said that, by setting sales records, it was also changing the country music business. Country singers were feeling freer to follow their spirits rather than the old formulas. Waylon and I saw this as a good thing. If we were at the forefront of a movement that meant more artistic autonomy, great.

Paul, though, took it a little literally. He knew that me and Waylon were hardly outlaws. We were pickers and singers and writers of songs. The only outlaw among us was Paul himself. He had earned the title. We hadn't. We got the label through the world of publicists. He got the label through the world of reality.

Wasn't much of an argument that day, though, because me and Waylon weren't about to debate the point. Part of Paul's mystique was his history as an outlaw. He was proud of his past. Proud to have survived, and proud to have maneuvered his way from the world of criminals to the world of musicians. He'd become a musician—and a damn good one.

"Ain't but one drummer, hoss," Waylon said, "who could play behind a man with the timing of a broken clock."

"The clock ain't broken," Paul pushed back. "It's just telling Texas time. Moving out here to Tennessee, you might be telling time a little differently."

"Everyone thinks Texas is the hot ticket right now," Waylon said. "Chips Moman just gave me this song he wrote with Bobby Emmons. He thinks it's a smash. Probably is. But I don't like it."

"What's it called?" asked Paul.

"'Luckenbach, Texas.'"

"Chips or Bobby ever been there?" Paul wanted to know.

"Nope."

"How 'bout you, Waylon?"

"Nope."

"Well, I been there," Paul said. "I suspect Willie has too."

"Sure have," I said. "It's just sixty or seventy miles west of Austin. It's where Jerry Jeff Walker cut his *Viva Terlingua* record. Luckenbach was good to Jerry Jeff."

"Well, maybe Willie should sing it," Waylon said.

"Let's hear it," I said.

Waylon picked up his guitar, placed a sheet of lyrics in front of him, and sang:

Let's go to Luckenbach, Texas
With Waylon and Willie and the boys
This successful life we're livin'
Got us feuding like the Hatfields and McCoys

"What do you think?" Waylon asked us.

"I think it's a hit," Paul said. "And I think Willie should sing it too."

"What do you think, Willie?" Waylon wanted to know.

"The writers gave it to you," I said. "Go on and cut it."

"I think it's too corny," Waylon said. "I think it's exploiting this whole Waylon/Willie thing."

"I hear it as a hit," Paul said. "Pretty melody. Good feeling."

"I like how it calls out Mickey Newbury and Hank Williams," I said. "I think it's got soul."

"So, you're telling me to record it, Willie?"

"Why not?"

"I'm feeling like all you guys are going to wind up singing it," Paul said.

And Paul was right. Waylon recorded it and had me sing on the closing refrain. "Luckenbach" sailed up the charts. Big hit for Waylon. Plus, I can't even count the times Waylon and I sang it together on stages the world over. Thanks to Waylon and the boys, little Luckenbach got famous.

★

Jim Keltner is a famous drummer who has recorded with everyone from Bob Dylan to John Lennon to Barbra Streisand to John Lee Hooker, not to mention Brian Wilson, Neil Young, and Mick Jagger. Producers and fellow musicians consider him *the* drummer of his generation, a virtuoso who can play in any style.

Waylon was the one who told Paul, "Jim Keltner has been coming to your gigs."

"Are you saying that to make me nervous?" Paul asked.

"Hell no. He's coming to your gigs to learn from you."

"Now I know you're messing with me."

"You're paranoid, Paul."

"I'm the least paranoid guy you'll ever meet. I'm not doing drugs."

"You don't have to do drugs to get paranoid. I'm telling you, Paul, Keltner loves the way you play."

All this happened before a show in Austin that Waylon and I were coheadlining. I figured it was time for me to put in my two cents.

"I'm not one to blow smoke up anyone's ass, Paul," I said, "but Waylon's right. Keltner talked to me about you."

"What'd he say?" Paul asked.

"You don't have enough sugar in your coffee, hoss?" Waylon asked Paul. "You really need more?"

"He told me that he comes to every Willie Nelson show he can," I said, "just to hear what you're doing."

"All I'm doing is following you," Paul said.

"And that's the trick of tricks," Waylon said. "One fool following another fool when the first fool doesn't even know where he's going."

I laughed and said, "Jim also said he'd love to play with us anytime we ask him."

"I hope you agreed," Paul said.

"I thanked him, of course," I said. "I told him that it'd be great. But then I thought—I already have a drummer. Better not take any chances."

"Willie's right," Waylon said. "Keltner is in awe of you 'cause of how much you can do with so little."

"That's an insult," Paul snapped.

"Hell no," I said. "It's the ultimate compliment. Far as I'm concerned, best compliment you can give a drummer is that you don't even know he's there. You don't hear him. You feel him."

"Amen," Waylon said.

For all Paul's confidence, he wasn't prideful or boastful about his drumming. He felt lucky to be playing with us. That's probably because his brother Oliver was the family musical genius. That's also why this conversation with me and Waylon meant so much to him. He didn't realize the uniqueness of his gift. But when we pointed out that a drummer like Jim Keltner was telling us that even he couldn't do what Paul did, the statement sunk in.

Waylon put his arm around Paul's shoulders and said, "Hoss, when Willie gives up this music thing and goes back to pig farming, you always got a gig with me."

Paul broke out into that smile of his. All was right with the world.

NEW YORK

Winter 1973

ME AND PAUL WERE WALKING down Broadway and wound up in Times Square. This was before Times Square became Disneyland and was still Smutland. Pimps and porn ruled the street. It was cold as hell.

"Hey, Rodeo Rick!" Paul hailed a bulky middle-aged man wearing a cowboy hat, a brown suede jacket with fringes, Lee jeans, and ostrich-skin boots. "What the hell are you doing around here?"

"Same thing we were doing in Hell's Half Acre in Fort Worth. Difference is, the money's better here. But the girls are meaner, and half the johns are cops looking for a free lay."

"You've always had good relations with the law," Paul said.

"Up here those relations cost an arm and leg," he said, turning to me. "Hey, Willie, last I saw you was at some joint over on Jacksboro Highway. You playing up here now?"

"Making a record."

"Well, I'll be the first to buy it."

"Thanks."

"Good to see you representing our hometown," Paul told Rodeo Rick. "Good to see that this rotten apple of a city hasn't scared you off."

"Oh, I don't scare off easy. And if I recall rightly, neither do you, Paul."

I vaguely remembered Rodeo Rick as a character from Paul's notorious past. Felt strange, though, having this conversation, the three of us standing in front of a Forty-Second Street movie theater that had a poster advertising: "Linda Lovelace in *Deep Throat*. How far does a girl have to go to untangle her tingle?"

The three of us started moseying down the street lined with one movie theater after another, the marquees blasting titles like *The Devil in Miss Jones* and *Behind the Green Door.*

"Tell me more about your record, Willie," Rick said.

"Not much to tell. Haven't started yet."

"Well, if you write a song as good as that 'Crazy' song you wrote for Patsy Cline, you can buy yourself a Park Avenue penthouse. I spent all last year listening to that song when I fell in love with one of my working ladies."

"That's a cardinal sin in your business," Paul said.

"Sure is. But Willie's song got me through. Hope you write another one like that on your new record, Willie."

"I don't see that happening," I said as we stopped in front of an adult shop where the window was crowded with sex toys.

"How come?" Rodeo Rick asked.

"It's a gospel record."

"Well, praise the Lord, Willie," Paul's pal from the old days said.

"That's just what we'll be doing," I said.

★

And that's what we did, under the strangest circumstances imaginable. RCA had dropped me like a bad habit. I had no record label when, by chance, Paul and I met Jerry Wexler, one of the owners of Atlantic Records, at a party in Nashville. This was the same producer who'd signed Doug Sahm and worked with everyone from Ray Charles to Aretha Franklin. Jerry was brimming with enthusiasm. He was as New York as pastrami on rye.

"This isn't your territory," I said. "What brings you to Nashville?"

"We're opening a sales office here, and I want to sign you," Jerry explained.

"Just like that?"

"Just like that. Nashville crucified you. I'm here to resurrect you."

"Glad you're talking that way, Jerry, because what I have in mind is a gospel record."

"Great."

"You got no objections? You're not worried about sales?"

"My only worry is that you'll keep cutting records where the producer is in charge. You're one of those artists, Willie, who was born to produce yourself. My job is stay out of the way. I have only one caveat."

"What's that?"

"Record in our studio in midtown Manhattan."

"Not here in Nashville?"

"You've recorded yourself to death in Nashville," Jerry said. "New York is new territory for you. You've never cut a record there, have you?"

"Never been asked to."

"I'm asking."

And before I could get out another word, Paul broke in to say, "He's accepting."

"I like your drummer," Jerry said. "Bring him to New York. Bring whoever you want. You provide the musicians, and I'll provide the electricity."

It happened so fast that, later in the evening when Jerry had left the party, I told Paul, "I've never seen you accept an offer like that before."

"I've never met a record man like him before. It isn't that he likes you, Willie. He loves you. He knows that you've had your hands tied. All he wants to do is untie them."

"He wants us to start recording in February. February is freezing in New York. That cape isn't going to do you much good."

"I'll buy a wool one."

★

From the funk of Times Square we made a beeline to high-society Saks Fifth Avenue where watching Paul pick out wool capes was a quite a sight. The upper-crust customers and snotty salesmen didn't know what to make of him—Paul in his black Stetson cowboy hat, black shirt, black jeans, and, just to give New York a thrill for their money, black elephant-hide boots with white stitching.

"These capes are usually worn for gala openings at the Metropolitan Opera or the New York City Ballet," the man in charge of formal wear said.

"I'm wearing it to a rodeo," Paul shot back.

"Oh, I see," the salesman said.

"I'll take the cashmere one."

"I think it's a bit long on you, sir."

"That's the whole point, buddy. It's what I want, as long as you can get your tailor to line it in red silk."

"Red silk?"

"Bloodred."

"I'll call the tailor."

Turned out the tailor was an elderly lady who grew up in Waco. She couldn't believe it was me and Paul standing there in the formal wear department. She told me that she liked my music, but her real hero was Hank Williams. I said, "Mine too."

She said she'd have the lining sewn in by the next day.

By the time we had our first session at Atlantic, Paul was wearing the cape. It was an especially memorable occasion because, after two decades, Bobbie was finally playing piano behind us. More than that, I had Bobbie pick out the gospel songs and write the arrangements. "Precious Memories," "In the Garden," "Will the Circle Be Unbroken"—all the songs we'd sung as kids at Abbott Methodist Church.

Paul's assessment of Jerry Wexler was right. Unlike other producers, Jerry didn't have a single stipulation. I got to use my own band. I didn't hear a word about outside studio musicians. In addition to the traditional gospel songs, I wrote a new song called "The Troublemaker." When I told Paul the title, he thought it was about him.

"It's about Jesus," I explained.

"Close enough." He laughed.

The song compared how the hippies were demonized as troublemakers to the treatment that Jesus received in his day.

Jerry, a proud New York Jew, said it was his favorite tune on the record. (Years later, he produced two of Bob Dylan's Jesus albums, *Slow Train Coming* and *Saved*.)

Jerry also wanted more. Since we were already up in New York, he surmised, why not do a session of secular songs?

"Write an original," Jerry urged.

"Don't have any originals right now," I admitted.

"Something will come to you. I reserved the studio time. Take as long as you need."

Like every writer, I can get stuck. Stuck in my hotel room, looking at the walls, I realized I had already written that song—"Hello Walls." No point in retreading an old tire.

Paul called.

"What are you doing, Willie?"

"I should be writing, but nothing's coming to mind."

"Something will. Something always does."

"I'm getting antsy. Doing nothing but sitting around in my underwear."

"Sounds like you got yourself the first line."

"You think people want to hear about me sitting around in my underwear?"

"I think people want to hear whatever's on your mind."

I shrugged. "If you say so."

I just started writing whatever came to mind. I called myself "Shotgun Willie" because of the incident with Lana's husband in Ridgetop. *Shotgun Willie sits around in his underwear.* Okay, what's next? *Bitin' on a bullet and pullin' out all of his hair. Shotgun Willie's got all his family there.* Guess I was remembering that time Paul shot up the Firebird belonging to my daughter's husband. Anyway, I didn't want to go into the whole story, so I switched gears.

I didn't have anything to say—which is just what I wound up saying. *You can't make a record if you ain't got nothing to say. You can't play music if you don't know nothing to play.*

Then I remembered how Paul and I had been reminiscing the other day about John T. Floore, who owned a joint outside San Antonio. Big John had once sold sheets to the Klan.

I thought about him selling those sheets on the family plan. Nice rhyme. John T.'s story really had nothing do with anything else in the song, but I thought it was a funny line. So, I stuck it in there.

"Shotgun Willie" was a shotgun song. Scattered shots. Scattered thoughts. Fragments that stuck together, or maybe they didn't. What would Jerry Wexler say?

"I'm putting it out," he said. "If you're okay with it, I'm calling the album *Shotgun Willie.*"

I was okay with it. In fact, I was so okay I wrote another song about a previous trip me and Paul had taken to New York. Called it "Devil in a Sleepin' Bag" because of this picture in my mind: Paul was in our broken-down bus in a sleeping bag, shivering because the heat wasn't working on a freezing-cold night.

We were headed home to Austin
Caught pneumonia on the road
Taking it home to Connie and the kids
A wheel ran off and jumped a railroad
Then ran through a grocery store
If you want to buy a bus, I'm taking bids

And the devil shivered in his sleeping bag

The song goes on to remember how me and Paul saw Kris Kristofferson and Rita Coolidge singing at Philharmonic Hall. I remember Rita singing like an angel. I called it "raw perfection there for all the world to see." Yet on that disastrous ride back, the memory wasn't enough to keep me sane. It was the sight of Paul, in his black cape, shivering in the sleeping bag. I called him the devil because that was the image that caught on. He might have been shivering but always stayed strong. He was the stalwart that kept our crazy boat afloat, even when it looked like it was drowning.

★

We made it back safely from New York to Austin. Paul and I were feeling pretty good about this new record.

"You know, Willie," Paul said. "With Bobbie in the studio and in your band, we really are like a family."

"We are a family," I said, bewildered by the *like*. "We are family. We just are."

We sighed and let the truth hang in the air like mist.

I'd been looking for a new band name, and there it was. Family. Family said it all. Fifty years later, the name's the same. Family is the currency that never devalues. Family is beyond value. The priceless thing that enriches our lives and our work.

Family extended when Paul invited a twenty-one-year-old harmonica player named Mickey Raphael to sit in with us in a high school gym at a benefit we were playing for the Lancaster, Texas, volunteer fire department. Mickey had been introduced to me by Darrell Royal, my close friend who coached the University of Texas championship football team in Austin. A big music fan, Darrell said Mickey could play. When Mickey showed up, Paul was gracious but honest. He told Mickey, "This isn't a paying gig tonight." Eager to show what he could do, Mickey couldn't have cared less. He played, and he stayed—for the next half century.

Mickey played so beautifully that I invited him to join us at our next New York gig, Max's Kansas City, a high-profile hipster club that booked everyone from the Velvet Underground to Patti Smith. To get ready, Mickey sat in with us at

Big G's, a rough redneck joint in Round Rock just outside Austin. Because Mickey's hair was longer and curlier than Harpo Marx's, Paul met him at his car and escorted him inside. Paul wanted to make certain that none of the anti-counterculture clowns messed with him.

During a break Mickey, a tall handsome guy, caught the eye of a fine young lady and struck up a conversation. After the gig, the gal accompanied Mickey to his car. Because Paul watched over everyone in the Family, he spotted a man following Mickey and his new friend. Paul figured the guy might be the lady's boyfriend. He figured right. The guy was about to murder Mickey when Paul's .45 fostered him to change his mind.

"Son," Paul schooled Mickey, "just because she tells you yes doesn't mean she hasn't told someone else the same thing. And if you're not on the lookout for that someone else, your ass is grass." And that was that.

TEXAS WORLD SPEEDWAY

Summer 1973

BECAUSE SOME TEN THOUSAND folks had turned out for that festival in Dripping Springs, Paul and I figured we could put on a festival of our own. Instead of doing it over two or three days, we decided to do it on one day: the Fourth of July.

"Call it Willie Nelson's Fourth of July Picnic," Paul said.

"Think anyone will actually show up?"

"It they do, great. If they don't, we'll still have a blast."

No argument against that. The Picnic was on. The idea was simple: Leon Russell would rustle up the hippies, and I'd rustle up the rednecks. By then, though, it was tough telling the two apart. The bill was a combination of old school—Loretta Lynn and Charlie Rich—and new school—Kris and Rita and Doug Sahm. The crowd was slow to arrive, making us nervous, but they finally wandered their way onto the seven-thousand-acre ranch. Weed was everywhere and so was beer. Didn't know or care how many fans were tripping on acid. All I knew was that everyone was loving the music. Goodwill won the day.

On the less miraculous side of things, the promoters we hired to sell tickets skimmed so much off the top we barely wound up breaking even. Paul wanted to carve up the promoters with a hunting knife, but I stopped him.

"It was an experiment that turned out good," I told Paul. "I believe we can turn it into a yearly thing. No need to bust any heads over it now. Next year you can bust as many heads as you like."

Next year Paul came up with the idea of holding the second annual Fourth of July Picnic at the Texas World Speedway. It was wild. Nitty Gritty Dirt Band. Greezy Wheels. An RV race around the speedway. More car wrecks than I care to remember, not to mention a couple of cars catching fire. Massive audience. Huge success. But when it came time to count the receipts, same story as the first year. Promoters pocketing profits. This time I gave Paul the okay to bust as many heads as necessary. But when they saw Paul coming, head-busting wasn't necessary. His reputation preceded him. Thanks to Paul, the promoters coughed up enough for us to squeeze out a small profit. That was good enough for me. The Picnic was more about music than money.

One of the most challenging Picnics required Paul to save the day. In Liberty Hill the sky cracked open, and rain came thundering down. Not to be defeated, we put a giant tarp over the stage. As the day went on, the rain worsened until the tarp was weighed down with so much water that we were certain it would collapse. Paul corrected the problem by pulling out his gun and blasting a hole in the rear section of the tarp. That drained the rainwater so we could keep playing while the crowd danced in the mud.

Despite the weather, it turned out to be a beautiful chapter in the history of our Picnics.

★

I called the last album I made for Jerry Wexler *Phases and Stages*. It coincided with the darkest phase in Paul's life.

I wrote it as a story based on the breakup of a romantic relationship. The man tells his side of the story, and the woman tells hers. The overall theme is sadness and loss. I was a little worried that Jerry might find it too depressing.

"The truth doesn't depress me," he said. "Go on and cut the record."

I did two versions with two different bands. Jerry suggested I go to Muscle Shoals and use his guys. They were great. But I also recorded the songs with my guys, Mickey on harp, Bee on bass, Jody Payne on guitar, Bobbie on piano, and, of course, Paul on drums.

I didn't see the record as personal. I wasn't feeling down. I wasn't having problems with Connie. And my career was going strong. My musical mind was simply imagining the heartbreak we all go through when we lose someone we love. None of it was personal—except for one song, the song that, looking back, I treasure most. It was a song written for my dear friend Paul.

Some months before we started recording, we were in Austin. There was an empty lot between the duplex where I lived with Connie and Paula and the duplex where Paul lived with Carlene and Darrell Wayne. Connie and Carlene had become best friends. Our families could not have been closer. Our lives were moving in a positive direction. Then on the morning of January 5, 1973, everything changed. Our world came crashing down.

I was still asleep. Connie was in the kitchen making breakfast when Darrell Wayne, then a teenager, came running over, crying and banging on our glass door. “Mom! Mom! It’s Mom!” He couldn’t stop screaming. I jumped out of bed, and Connie and I ran over to Paul’s. I’d never seen such an expression on Paul’s face. He whispered the words. They were barely audible. I didn’t want to believe what I’d heard. He knew that, so he repeated them. It took all his strength to do so. “Carlene’s shot herself.” The bathroom door was half open. I could see the blood. I asked Connie to take Darrell Wayne back to our house. I stayed with Paul and helped him make the calls he needed to make. We sat next to each other on the living room couch, waiting for the medics to arrive. There was nothing I could say that would help. None of us were even remotely prepared for the fact that Carlene had died by suicide. Even though I knew that her father had also died by suicide years earlier, Carlene herself had shown no signs of depression or mental stress. When I later asked Connie about it, she was as mystified as I was. In the aftermath of New Year’s Eve, Carlene had seemed perfectly fine. She and Paul were having no problems. She was a devoted mother and a devoted wife. And yet, at age thirty-three, she was gone.

A psychiatrist later told me that the propensity for literal self-destruction is often genetic. He put it in layman’s terms. “We understand how heart attacks can assault us,” he said, “but brain attacks are more mysterious. Suicides can be seen as brain attacks. The circuitry implodes, and the pain is too great to bear. You feel that the only way out—the only relief—is to end it all.”

★

Words are words, and explanations are explanations, but this was a time when language was beside the point. Paul was inconsolable. It didn't matter that he was the strongest dude I'd ever known. It didn't matter that he feared no one. It didn't matter that, before this, he had weathered every kind of storm. This was different. This brought my brother Paul to his knees.

Paul was a thinker, a mathematician, a marksman, a strategist, a loyalist. Paul was a hundred different things, but he wasn't a songwriter or a singer. Because of that, and because I felt so close to him, I decided to do for him what he couldn't do for himself. In writing a song about his precious Carlene, I decided to become him. I wrote as if I were Paul and called it "I Still Can't Believe You're Gone."

I write songs quickly. I let my heart do the thinking. My heart's a better thinker than my mind. It's also a quicker thinker. I write simple words and simple melodies. If I get too fancy, I lose my focus. My focus was on Carlene and the pain of her passing.

I wanted Paul to hear the song before anyone else. When I wrote "Me and Paul" and "Devil in a Sleepin' Bag" I'd had no doubt that Paul would like the songs. The first was an homage to our brotherhood, and the second was a tribute to the guise he loved to embody. But "I Still Can't Believe You're Gone" was different. In the other songs I was expressing my feelings. In this one I was expressing his. Maybe that was presumptuous. Maybe Paul didn't want to say the things I was singing about. Maybe I was getting too personal.

So, before doing anything else, I went over to see Paul, who was doing his best to comfort Darrell Wayne. He made us some coffee, and we sat around the kitchen table. Since the death of Carlene, Paul had turned painfully quiet. He had turned off that nonstop storytelling machine that made him so special. He was covered in grief.

"Got something I want you to hear, Paul," I said.

He just nodded.

"It's about Carlene."

He nodded again.

"Wrote a song about her."

"I like that. That was good of you, Willie."

"Except I wrote it differently than I usually write. I wrote it pretending I was you. Before I play it for anyone else, I want you to hear it. It's okay if you don't like it. You won't hurt my feelings. I'll just forget the whole thing."

"Go on and play it then."

I picked up my guitar and sang:

This is the very first day since you left me
But I've tried to put my thoughts in a song
And all I can hear myself singin' is
I still can't believe you're gone
. . . There's just too many unanswered questions . . .

. . . I don't like it
But I'll take it till I'm strong . . .
And I still can't believe you're gone

When I was through, tears flowed from Paul's eyes. He tried to talk but couldn't.

"You don't have to say anything," I said.

"I want to say something, Willie."

"What's that?"

"Thank you."

"I Still Can't Believe You're Gone" became part of *Phases and Stages*. It's my favorite song on that record. Nearly fifty years later, I'm still singing it.

★

When Atlantic closed down their country music division, Jerry Wexler protected me. He got me out of my deal because he knew the label wouldn't give me the promotion I needed. That led to a new contract with Columbia, one of the biggest record companies in the world. Only one problem: unlike Jerry, the execs at Columbia were hesitant about granting me artistic freedom.

Even though Paul was still in deep mourning over Carlene, he didn't miss a beat. Didn't miss a show. And as this Columbia confrontation was coming down, he stood by my side. "Demand artistic freedom," he said. "Don't sign the contract unless it says you can do whatever you want to do."

"I'm not sure they'll accept that."

"I am. I'm telling you, Willie, at this point there's no looking back. They're going to give you free rein."

They did, but they still weren't happy. When I turned in the record, they thought it was a demo. Said it was too rough. Too crude. Told me to do it over. Again, I took Paul's advice: "It's not their record. It's yours."

I called the record *Red Headed Stranger*, and, admittedly, it was strange.

"You're doing that song I first heard you sing when you were on KCNC back home, the one you sang to Lana?" Paul asked.

"The same."

"What else?"

"A bunch of nonsense."

"Your nonsense always makes sense."

"To you."

"To most everyone."

"We'll see whether people like these old songs. Actually, some are new."

"Actually, all that matters, Willie, is that you like them."

I did. *Red Headed Stranger* started out inside my head as a film on a big screen. I saw it as a big story. The first song starts talking about the time of a preacher. He loves a lady so deeply he goes mad. He cries like a baby and screams like a panther and then, in the year of our Lord 1901, heads out into the night. But then my story gets more abstract. It goes from the song "Denver," which I wrote after a skiing trip, and winds up in "Bandera," where me, Paul, and our tribe lived before moving to Austin. Along the way, I included old songs that seemed to fit the mood, like "Blue Eyes Crying in the Rain," which was written by Fred Rose and recorded by Roy Acuff in the mid-1940s. I loved the lyrics about meeting up yonder and strolling hand in hand in a land that knows no parting. The song touched my heart.

"The album is incoherent," the Columbia execs said. "It doesn't jell. And besides, all you've done is give us demo tapes."

"These aren't demo tapes," I said. "This is the finished product."

They said I was crazy.

"You are crazy," Paul said. "Crazy enough to put this thing out as is. I wouldn't change a note."

Paul was emotionally invested because it was him and Mickey Raphael who'd found Autumn Sound, an out-of-the-way studio in Garland, Texas, where we cut the tunes. Columbia wanted us recording in Nashville. I said no.

Columbia also said they'd give us a $60,000 recording budget. I said fine and recorded the album for $2,000. Columbia demanded that we rerecord the album because it sounded too sparse. I said I wanted it sparse. Columbia said they wouldn't put it out. I said, "You got no choice. My contract gives me control."

Though they were certain it'd flop, Columbia put the album out. Instead of flopping, it flew. "Blue Eyes Crying in the Rain" went all the way up to number one. *Red Headed Stranger* went gold. And nothing was ever the same.

Paul's first wife, Carlene.

AUSTIN

Winter 1973

"PAUL WILL NEVER BE THE SAME." That's what Bee Spears said. Bee was nearly as close to Paul as I was. Bass players and drummers have a special relationship. Together, they bring rhythm to life. If they're not in sync, the rhythm isn't right. Paul and Bee were always in sync. Bee, by the way, had a dead-on impression of Paul's distinctively nasal voice.

"Sooner or later," I said to Bee, "he'll find himself."

"He wasn't ready for what happened to Carlene."

"No one's ever ready for something like that."

"But Paul's a guy who's always been able to control the circumstances of his life. You know that better than me, Willie. You know how things have always worked out right for him. But there's no righting this. I'm really worried about him."

"We all are," I said. "But we all know what's best for him."

"What *is* best for him?"

"To leave him alone. He knows he can come talk to any of us whenever he wants to. But he also knows we're not going to bother him. We're not to suffocate him with pity. That's the last thing he needs."

"So, what do you think he needs?"

"To keep doing what he's doing. Getting on that bus. Making every gig. Playing the drums. Keeping our books. Taking care of Darrell Wayne. Now more than ever, Paul needs the routine. He needs the Family."

★

We were all thinking of ways to help Paul get through this devastation. When a brother is hurting so bad, you desperately want to comfort him. Connie was the one who came up with a beautiful idea.

At the time, she was driving a black 1972 T-Bird with a black leather interior that Paul loved. He never tired of praising that car.

"Why don't we give it to him?" Connie asked me.

"Let's do it," I said.

When we handed him the keys, he wouldn't accept.

"It's too much," he said.

"You love that damn car a lot more than Connie does," I said.

"And you'll enjoy driving it a lot more than I ever will," Connie added.

Paul couldn't argue. He knew we were speaking the truth. All he could do was wipe the tears from his eyes.

★

His dark days dragged on. He suffered but soldiered his way through. To beat back the blues, he had some wild times, but that was to be expected. That wildness, though, had its limits. He still never missed a gig or failed to fulfill his responsibilities as band member and bookkeeper. In his grief, he remained a great drummer and great friend. He hung in.

Eventually, music's healing powers worked their wonders.

His good-hearted nature never waned. I'm thinking about his somewhat suspect second "marriage" that resulted from his good heart. He knew a woman who needed help—there was a custody issue with her children—and, as a favor, "married" her onstage at our Fourth of July Picnic. I put "married" in quotes because the man officiating had a mail-order preacher's license. Didn't matter. Paul was dead set on coming to the aid of a lady in distress, and so the ceremony took place.

He thought that once the good deed was done, he'd be a free man. But the woman took the marriage far more seriously than Paul and, in fact, moved into an apartment in the same Austin complex where Paul lived. She wouldn't leave poor Paul alone. Things got so intense that Paul had to up and quit Austin. Along with his son Darrell Wayne, he skipped out in the middle of the night. That's how they wound up living the high life in Dallas.

Paul and Janie shortly after they got married, c. 1980.

TURTLE CREEK

1976

IT'S ABOUT FORTY MILES FROM Jacksboro Highway in Fort Worth to Turtle Creek in Dallas. As a young man, Paul gained his reputation along Jacksboro Highway. As a middle-aged man, Paul planted his flag in Turtle Creek. Jacksboro Highway was down and dirty. Turtle Creek was super swanky. To escape his so-called second "wife," Paul had moved into an exclusive high-rise overlooking the Kalita Humphreys Theater, an architectural landmark designed by Frank Lloyd Wright.

"It's a party apartment," Paul liked to say.

This was a period when, still mourning for Carlene, Paul looked to ease the pain through heavy partying.

One party took a strange turn. He told me the story when we were on my bus, the *Honeysuckle Rose*, crossing the Oklahoma border into Missouri.

"Happened in Dallas last Saturday night," he said. "Me and a few friends had been over at a bowling alley on Harry

Hines Boulevard that day." Paul, by the way, was an ace bowler. "That afternoon we'd won some good money off a crew of hotshots who came down from Denton to clean up. I'm not bragging . . ."

"Sure you are," I said. "Go on and brag."

"Well, the truth, Willie, is that I had three straight games over two hundred seventy. I was in the zone and decided to have everyone back at the apartment to celebrate. I didn't do a thing—no drugs, no drinks—but my friends were feeling pretty good, so we decided to take the party out to the park across the street for a nighttime picnic. It was a beautiful evening. Full moon. Soft summer breeze. Fireflies floating around. Got us some folding chairs so we could sit by Turtle Creek.

"We had us a portable grill and were cooking up a mess of sausages and burgers and corn on the cob when a line of limos pulled up. Turned out it was opening night of some play at the Dallas Theater Center and the fancy folks from that exclusive Dallas Country Club just up the road were arriving. Wearing tuxes, the men looked like penguins. The women were decked out in diamonds and sparkly gowns. A couple of the younger gals might have had too many martinis at the country club because when they smelled the weed my boys were smoking, they trotted on over. I guess they figured our picnic might be more fun than some boring play. So, there we were, laughing and giggling and taking a toke or two. That didn't sit well with their gussied-up men friends. The guys started objecting, but the gals had minds of their own. They wanted to party with us. One of the bigger dudes headed in my direction and asked what was going on.

"'Just a peaceful picnic in the park,' I said.

"'Clear out!' he demanded.

"'You own this park?'

"'Clear the hell out!' he repeated.

"'Well, sir,' I said, 'given that we're both standing on public property, I figure I have as much right to be here as you.'

"'I'm calling the police,' he said.

"'Before doing that, I suggest you cool off.'

"'I'm not cooling off, and I'm not backing off.'

"'Then let me give you a hand.' With that, I picked up the son of a bitch and threw him in Turtle Creek. The gals laughed hysterically. The man turned out to be a good swimmer. He climbed out of the creek, swearing that the cops would clear us out. But the cops must have had something better to do because they never turned up. We ate our sausages and burgers and corn on the cob, and after a while we took the party back up to my apartment."

"And the ladies in the evening gowns?" I asked.

"They partied harder than you can imagine."

"Oh, I can imagine," I said.

★

"The Party's Over" was the name of a song I wrote down in Houston around the same time I composed "Crazy" and "Funny How Time Slips Away." That was the '50s. Now it was the '70s, and I was thinking that, far as my songwriting went, the party might well have been over—at least for a while. Like I said before, I can't force songs. They either show up or they don't. None had shown up for a good spell.

I am not going to credit Paul for my next musical move. But I do have to remember something Paul said to me that I had never heard before.

"Willie," he said, "I'm in love."

The statement shocked me. Paul was a lot of things. But the devil shivering in his sleeping bag was *not* a man who suddenly announced that he was in love. Since Carlene had passed, Paul had had his fair share of girlfriends. Women were crazy about him. But his women were here today, gone tomorrow. As far as romance went, Paul English remained unattached. Until he met a woman named Janie Gray.

"Janie let the light in," Paul said. "She's brilliant. She's smart and sexy and full of life. She loves to laugh. Her spirit reignited my spirt. Janie sees right to the bottom of my soul. And it doesn't scare her. She keeps saying she's never met anyone like me. I say the same about her."

Paul and Janie met in 1977 and married in 1979.

"Deep down in my bones," Paul told me, "I know she's the love of my life."

Janie tells it like this:

"I was living in Dallas and met Paul, easily the most fascinating man I had ever encountered, through my friend Mickey Raphael, who mentioned that he needed a ride to the Athens Black-Eyed Pea Festival. I volunteered. We drove down there—about seventy miles—and when we arrived, Mickey said, 'Feel free to hang around if you'd like to.' Just about then I noticed a man getting out of black Thunderbird. He had this presence, this mystique. I wasn't shy. I asked Mickey, 'Would you mind introducing me to that guy?'

"'I'd love to,' Mickey said. 'That's Paul English.'

"Right off, Paul engaged me in conversation. He wasn't flirtatious as much as he was curious. Wanted to know everything about me. Well, I wanted to know everything about him. But, as I would soon learn, that would take years. All I knew was that I felt drawn to him. The attraction was powerful. In no time, we became a couple. He put up with my feistiness. I put up with his idiosyncrasies. He let me into his mind and into his world. I was eager to enter.

"I was enrolled in Richland College and working in a Garland medical center as an EEG technician in the psychiatric practice of Dr. Joe Black whose specialty was neurodiagnostics. Human behavior has always fascinated me. A lifetime later, I'd earn two master's degrees—one in sociology and another in counseling psychology. But when I met Paul, I had yet to complete my education. My salary was minimal, and I lived in a crappy apartment off Coit Road. Paul didn't mind. He loved staying over. He'd show up with a couple of pistols and bags filled with money—the revenue for the shows that he demanded in cash—and did the paperwork for the band's salary on my little desk.

"When he learned that it was my twenty-second birthday, he got together a group and took us to a strip club on Greenville Avenue. I thought that was novel. I thought it was hilarious. I thought it was very Paul. It was only when all the strippers knew him by name that I felt obliged to ask him why. 'Everyone knows me by name,' he replied. And, as it turned out, everyone did.

"Now here's a strange paradox. Though it's fair to describe Paul as a dangerous character, someone who lived outside the boundaries of normal behavior, no one I knew feared him. Everyone loved him. I know he had a long history of enemies, but his list of friends outnumbered his adversaries a hundred to one.

"He also had remarkable strength of mind. We were once in Vegas at the blackjack table. Paul had gone back to cigarettes, and the smoke was driving me crazy. It triggered my allergies and brought tears to my eyes.

"'I really can't stand it, Paul,' I said.

"'Fine,' he replied. He snuffed out his cigarette in an ashtray and never smoked again. Seeing how it bothered me was enough to make him stop. His willpower was absolute.

"Early on, I witnessed his devotion to Willie. That was also absolute. I was in the audience when they were onstage in

Houston. Someone threw a beer bottle that missed Willie by inches and came flying by Paul. I saw that Paul was able to identify the beer thrower, a big man in the second row. For the rest of the show, Paul never let the guy out of his sight. The second after Willie had sung his last song, Paul bolted from his drums and went after the bottle thrower. He caught him and punched him so hard that, in doing so, Paul broke his own hand. 'Doesn't matter,' Paul said. 'He got it worse than me.'

"When we got back to Dallas, I knew an orthopedic surgeon in the same Garland medical center. Reluctantly, Paul agreed to surgery. As soon as the operation was over and his hand was set in a cast, he wanted to go home. I couldn't pick him up on time because I was working. He couldn't wait. When I arrived at the hospital, he was already gone. No one knew where he was. I drove around and spotted him in a telephone booth next to a 7-Eleven. He was wearing a hospital gown along with red boots and a black cowboy hat. When he saw me, he kept chattering on the phone while he waved and smiled.

"'What in the world are you doing?' I asked when his call ended.

"'Doing Willie's business,' he said. 'Working out the logistics for our next gig.'

"'Couldn't you have done that in the hospital?' I asked.

"'They wouldn't let me use the phone. They said I had to rest.'

"'Well, don't you?' I asked.

"'Hell no. Never felt better.'

"At one point Paul had me fly out to Tahoe where the band was playing.

"'Why don't you quit your job and come out on the road with me for a while?' he asked.

"'If I did that,' I said, 'I'd probably need a wedding ring.'

"'No problem,' he said. It all seemed so whimsical. Laughing, we both said we'd be surprised if it lasted six months. Forty-two years later, we were still laughing."

★

Paul called his marriage to Janie the best move of his life. In his midforties, he settled down and became a family man. I believe that was something he also craved. He and Janie had two terrific boys, Paul Jr.—called RP—and Evan, and along with his son Darrell Wayne, they became the most important people in his life. He doted his love and attention on them. He even stopped cursing.

After meeting Janie, Paul said, "You know, Willie, a man gets tired of running around. You get to where you want to conserve your energy, when you want to spend a quiet evening with your sweetheart, cuddle up, and listen to those old love songs. There's nothing like those old love songs."

Those old songs had been much on my mind.

"Those old songs are going to ruin your outlaw reputation," one of the record label execs told me.

His attitude made me want to sing them even more.

First song I thought of was "Stardust," written in the 1920s by Hoagy Carmichael and Mitchell Parish. I'd been hearing it my whole life. Bing Crosby sang it. Frank Sinatra sang it. Nat King Cole sang it.

"More people have sung it than any song written in the twentieth century," the same exec said. "The song is sung and done. I cannot think of a worse choice."

Not only did I decide to record it, I named the album *Stardust*. During a summer vacation in Malibu, I'd met Booker T. Jones of Booker T. and the MG's. He turned out to be a great arranger/producer. Booker, Bobbie, and I picked out nine other standards from long ago and far away—songs like "Moonlight in Vermont" and "Blue Skies"—and did the album in seven days. No violins, no backup singers, just straight-ahead ballads with my bottom-line crew: Paul on drums, Mickey on harp, Bee on bass, Bobbie and Booker on keys, and Jody Payne on guitar.

When we got through, I told Paul, "At least you got some love songs you can take home and play for Janie."

"A lot more couples than just me and Janie are going to be listening to this."

Five million copies later, I couldn't argue. *Stardust* had more staying power than anything I'd ever recorded. The damn thing stayed on the bestselling music charts for ten years.

★

The party's over was a phrase I had heard in another context.

Most folks thought my Fourth of July Picnic would never become an annual event. I myself wasn't all that sure. Paul was. Paul was the guy who handled the shady characters looking to swindle the massive crowds growing larger every year. No matter the location—Dripping Springs or College Station, Liberty Hill or Gonzales—we made it through. I was spared the details. Frankly, I'm not that good at details. But Paul's keen sense of finance and gift for rooting out scumbag promoters made sure that, year after year, the party never died.

Gallons of ink have been employed by writers trying to capture the mood. Among my favorite description is Billy Porterfield's: "It was miserable and it was great, crazy and calm, funky and fun. It was one of the glorious heathen stomps between the Americas of J. Edgar Hoover, Joe McCarthy and Ronald Reagan. Many came the evening before and spent the night passing stories and hits around campfires. It felt holy and high. It was always a beautiful event."

There were fires in parking lots, nude swimming in hidden (and not-so-hidden) ponds, lawsuits by nervous neighbors, post-Picnic congratulatory notes from those same nervous neighbors when their fears proved unfounded, crowds numbering from twenty thousand to eighty thousand, $40,000 bills for port-o-cans, but, most importantly, there were memorable musical moments from Lynyrd Skynyrd, Johnny Paycheck, Neil Young, Jerry Jeff Walker, the Beach Boys, Jon Bon Jovi, Stevie Ray Vaughan, and old friends Roger Miller, Johnny Cash, Ray Price, and Faron Young—to name just a few.

One of the best spots for our Picnic turned out to be an old country club I'd bought thirty miles outside Austin called Pedernales.

"It's perfect for you," Paul said when he came to survey the property. "Got a nine-hole rocky golf course to go with your rocky golf game and enough land for you to build whatever you want—a house, a recording studio, even a corral for those rescue horses you love so much. You love 'em because you relate to 'em. You're something of a rescue horse."

I laughed and agreed. Bought the property. Made a home there. Built a studio. And played the hell out of that rocky golf course. In fact, some of the best times I shared with Paul were our legendary golf tournaments. We loved playing into early evening before recording in the studio late into the night.

It was at one at those sessions where, for all the trust I had in Paul, I was afraid that his attitude of taking no shit from anyone would ruin one of the relationships I cherished most.

MY STUDIO

Early '80s

HAVING MY VERY OWN PLACE to record birthed many blessings. I was blessed to be able to make music anytime, night or day. Blessed to have a home, family, and friends—not to mention a golf course—so close by. And blessed to be able to invite other artists to come in and work.

When I invited Ray Charles, I wasn't sure whether he'd accept. Aretha Franklin once called him "The Right Reverend Ray" because everything he did not only had a sacred sound but also was right. His singing, piano playing, even his saxophone playing, expressed the pain and joy of the human soul.

Ray was a rugged individualist. No one could "manage" him. Early on, he figured out the business and got control of his own masters. He owned the building where he worked. He owned his own plane. He did what he wanted to do when he wanted to do it. You couldn't pressure Ray into anything. Since I'd met him a lifetime earlier in Dallas, we'd often talked about recording together. I'd told him how his *Modern*

Sounds in Country and Western Music had been a game changer for artists like me. I know that Johnny Cash, Waylon, Kris, and Merle felt the same. Ray had not only infused country music with his own brand of burning soul but also expanded our audience. We had nothing but love for Ray, which he reciprocated. When the press questioned him, he'd mentioned me—along with Hank Williams, George Jones, and Conway Twitty—among his favorite singers. We had talked about doing a duet, but our schedules, crazy as they were, never coincided.

Then came the day I ran into him at the Atlanta airport. He was flying in, and I was flying out.

"Heard about your golf course, Willie," he said, "and golf's not my best game. But I can still whip your ass in chess, with the lights on and off. A little birdie also told me you also got a recording studio where you give your friends a discount as long as they don't outsing you. Any truth to any of that?"

"It's all true, Ray, and the studio is yours anytime you want it."

A song brought us together. Producer Billy Sherrill sent "Seven Spanish Angels" to both me and Ray. It had a Marty Robbins "El Paso" vibe, an epic feel. Written by Troy Seals and Eddie Setser, the story concerns a gunslinger and his girlfriend cornered by a posse who guns them down in cold blood. Their deaths are mourned by angels.

"We can record it anywhere," I said when Ray called me to express his eagerness to do it as a duet.

"The story takes place in Texas," Ray said. "The song has Texas written all over it. You're always bragging that you got the best studio in Texas, so I say let's do this thing in Texas."

I was thrilled. Ray was coming to Pedernales!

A week later, he was there. Five minutes after arriving, he said, "Good to see you, Willie."

Ray loved using the word *see.* He never saw his blindness as a deterrent.

"Now show me around that famous course of yours."

He took my arm as we walked around the first four holes.

"One day I'm gonna surprise you and take up this sport," he said.

"Nothing about you is gonna surprise me, Ray."

When we got to the studio, the engineer was having a problem with the board.

"Open this thing up," Ray said, "and let me take a look."

A first-rate mechanic of both car and airplane engines, Ray, who ran his own studio back in Los Angeles, gave the wiring a once-over and figured out what was wrong. My engineer shook his head in wonder.

Time to rehearse the tune. Naturally, Paul was on drums.

What we didn't know, but would soon learn, was that Ray was hell on drummers. Like me, Ray had idiosyncratic timing. In other words, he fooled with the beat, sometimes moving ahead, sometimes falling behind. Paul had been trained in this school of uneven phrasing by me. Intuitively, he understood my strange way of singing. But he wasn't used to Ray, and Ray wasn't used to him.

Because music was so visceral to Ray, the wrong drum accent would do more than throw him off; it would disturb him. And as a man who spoke his mind, he was quick to voice his disturbance.

"No!" he barked at Paul. "You're not following me!"

Paul tried again, and again the rhythm didn't hit Ray right.

"Watch my feet," Ray said. "Follow my feet."

Ray beat out the groove with his feet, but the groove was uneven. That unevenness was what made Ray, Ray. But it also made Paul a little crazy. It was an ever-changing groove.

I pause to give you a picture of two tough men:

Ray Charles, one of the great innovators of American music who'd earned the right, like Frank Sinatra, to do it his way.

And Paul English, up from the mean streets of Fort Worth, who, if spoken to unkindly, was capable of anything.

The rehearsal continued. Ray sang a verse. I sang a verse. Ray played piano. Mickey Raphael played harp. Ray sang a chorus. I sang a chorus. He and I sang a chorus together. And all the while, Ray stayed on Paul's case. He didn't let up.

Part of me was worried. After all, my favorite artist was telling my best friend (and favorite drummer) that he wasn't measuring up. My best friend carried a loaded pistol. My favorite artist was growing more irritable by the minute. It was not a happy situation. It could have even been a dangerous situation. *Should I intervene? If so, how? Who am I to tell Ray Charles to cool it? And, knowing Paul, what are the chances he'll cool off even if I ask him?*

I decided to do what Mama Nelson would have advised me to do. I prayed.

Dear Lord, let me keep my mouth shut so that these two tough hombres can work it out on their own.

Praise God, the prayer paid off. Much to Paul's credit, he never back-talked Ray but instead kept looking for that elusive groove. Finally, to Ray's satisfaction, he found it. I breathed a sigh of deep relief.

In peace and brotherhood, we rehearsed the song for another hour. We felt we had a masterpiece. "Seven Spanish Angels," as sung by me and Brother Ray, went on to be a number one hit. I considered it a milestone of my career and told Paul that I saw him in a totally different light.

"Well, aren't you the model of patience and restraint," I mused.

"It wasn't easy," Paul admitted. "I know he's a genius, but I came this close to taking a cymbal and hitting him over the head."

That same night Ray and I stayed up playing chess. Can't remember who won. Or maybe I don't want to remember. The following afternoon, Ray took his departure. Before getting in the car, he thanked me for my hospitality, looked around at all the acreage I'd acquired, and said, "Next time I'll be bringing my golf clubs."

Paul lifting his brush after a great set sometime in the '90s.

IMAGINARY MOUNT RUSHMORE

Beyond Time

JACK PROPP, A FINE DRUMMER himself, was mentored by Paul. He was one of the many drummers Paul helped along the way. I'm going to let Jack speak for himself:

"First time I saw Paul was at the Tulsa Memorial Auditorium in the midseventies. I was eighteen and a student at the Hank Thompson School of Country Music. I'd seen tub beaters before, but not like Paul. He was a striking figure. That jet-black razor-sharp goatee, those red patent leather boots. I felt, *This is as close as I'm going to get to seeing Elvis Presley.* Paul had that kind of charisma.

"Later down the road, a mutual friend, Cowboy Jack Melton, who was also close to Willie, introduced me to Paul. I asked him, 'Where's that snare you played on the album *San Antonio Rose*? Man, your snare work on that record was something else.'

"'Thank you,' he said, 'but the damn drum got burned up in a fire.'

"So I ran home, grabbed the exact snare he'd used—a Rogers Dyna-Sonic—and ran back to the band bus. 'Take mine,' I said.

"'You don't have to give me your drum,' he said.

"'Yes, I do,' I said. 'If it weren't for you, I wouldn't be a drummer.'

"We got to talking. He told me that his favorite drummer was Louie Bellson, 'The only white man in Duke Ellington's otherwise all-Black band.' Paul said, 'That's how good he was. The first to use two bass drums at the same time. He swung his ass off. I loved him so much I memorized his real name. Luigi Paulino Alfredo Francesco Antonio Balassoni. He was a superstar who married another superstar: Pearl Bailey. You might think it strange that a country drummer like me idolized a jazz drummer like Louie, but all drumming comes down to rhythm, and Louie had rhythmic genius. He also gave me the best advice I've ever received. Three words: *Less is more.*'

"I took Paul's advice to heart. The more I listened to him—especially his beautifully subtle work on Willie's *Stardust*—the more I realized that Paul played from the heart. He was all heart. He treated me, just a kid he'd met, with kindness and respect. His inspiration was so great that I made him a red drum seat with black piping and his initials.

"Paul had a mechanical mind. He was an inventor who didn't get credit for his originality and ingenuity. He came up with hot rod drumsticks. That's when he took wood dowels and glued them together. His invention. He said that when he played outdoor venues, his brush work—and Paul was mainly a brush man—couldn't be heard. He needed something heavier, but, always a master of subtlety, he invented the hot rods, a device halfway between a brush and a stick. Wider than a brush but softer than a stick. Listen to Willie's 'On the Road Again.' Or Charlie Daniels's 'The Devil Went Down to Georgia,' where you'll hear the drummer using Paul's invention.

"Right now, virtually every drummer has a pair of hot rods in his kit. Even though Paul was a strong personality, he wasn't a braggart. He never patented the idea or cared about credit. I cared. When years later someone else claimed it was his invention, I went public to tell the world that Paul English had invented hot rods way back in '83.

"After listening to Paul for a lifetime, I'm still amazed by his feel for time. Take 'Bloody Mary Morning.' Listen to the interplay between Paul, Willie, and Bee. Listen to how they're locked in. It's like a country version of the Allman Brothers Band.

"If someone builds a Mount Rushmore of country drummers, there will be five faces carved in stone: Fluke Holland from Johnny Cash, Biff Adam from Merle Haggard, Willie Cantu from Buck Owens, Richie Albright from Waylon Jennings, and Paul.

"It's fun to compare Richie and Paul. Richie was good with his bass drum. Paul was good with his high hat. I always said Richie was the Chevy Corvette and Paul the Caddy Eldorado.

"A veteran musician once told Paul, 'If I find someone who has your left foot and Richie's right foot, they'll be the perfect drummer.'

"'You wouldn't have to do that,' Paul said. 'The perfect drummer already exists.'

"'Who's that?'

"'My brother Billy.'

"That was Paul. Always ready to pass the praise on to others. And the truth is that Billy, Paul's younger brother, who has now played with Willie for years, did inherit Paul's greatness. I think Willie would agree."

Willie does agree. Over the course of a lifetime, my musicianship has been elevated by the presence of all three English brothers: Oliver, Paul, and Billy.

Paul is an upstanding citizen, until he's not.

And when he's not, watch out!

WAYLON JENNINGS

SOMEWHERE

Sometime

ALL WAS NOT RIGHT with the world.

Me and Paul had taken many trips. In fact, that's what the song "Me and Paul" is all about. But I took one kind of trip alone. And I'm not sure I would have survived if Paul hadn't been near.

I'm talking about LSD. When it came to mind-altering substances, I was always curious. I liked reading books on metaphysics. And though I was raised on the love ethos—and remain a believer—I also believe in reincarnation. Mainly, though, I believe in spiritual exploration. Open the heart. Open the mind. Somewhere in the far reaches of my memory, I recall Hamlet telling his pal, "There are more things in heaven and earth, Horatio, Than are dreamt of in your philosophy."[7] That's what I told my pal Paul before I went on my first and only acid trip.

"Where'd you get the stuff from?" Paul asked.

"A friend."

"You sure it's good?"

"He said it's the best."

"And you're sure you want to take it?"

"I'm curious. He called it a space exploration. Who doesn't want to explore space?"

A little while later, Paul approached me again.

"You sure you want to do this thing, Willie? We got a concert in two hours."

"I already took it."

"How much you take?

"A tab, I think they call it."

"Hell, man, you were supposed to take a third. A full tablet is going to send you into orbit."

"You're thinking like an accountant, Paul."

"I'm thinking you're going to be in no shape to do this show."

I was sure I had it all under control. But as time went on, I lost control. I damn near lost my mind. At first, it was all daisies and roses, fields of flowers, beautiful fragrances and lovely forms, everything and everyone connected. But then the vibe changed. When I got onstage, I felt disconnected from my body. Were those my hands? I could barely grab hold of Trigger. Started seeing bugs turning into buzzing little devils. Crazy stuff. Unsettling stuff. Wanted it all to end. Wanted to get off the spaceship and come back to Earth. But I came to learn that acid trips take as long as they take. You can't cut them off. You got to go the distance.

As my mind turned to mud, it was only by glancing back at Paul that was I able to keep my cool. Paul kept time to my LSD trip in a way that beat back the demons. He reined me in and saved me from sinking into a sea of insanity. When the show was over, Paul, Mickey, and Sister Bobbie formed a circle around me. In their faces I saw real love and concern.

Friendship, family, a feeling of safety. With their help, I got through the ordeal.

That hellacious trip convinced me that pot and pot alone was the only high I could trust. Pot never jacked me up too high or dropped me down too low. It kept me in the mellow middle. Other colleagues got cooked up on coke. I couldn't abide cocaine. I saw it as a drug that separates you from your soul. Fills you with false grandiosity. Turns pleasant folks into flaming assholes. I gave my band a directive: "If you're wired, you're fired."

★

By the time 1977 rolled around, Paul was not only my best friend but also my main advisor. He was the first to warn me that my then manager wasn't on the up-and-up. I was slow to act because, well, I'm a trusting guy. You could even say foolishly trusting. Back in Abbott, Mama and Daddy Nelson taught us to give folks the benefit of the doubt. Of course, Abbott was a small village where we took care of one another. Mama and Daddy Nelson knew little about the cold-blooded world. They were workers, amateur musicians, wonderful people but hardly sophisticated. They gave Sister Bobbie and me the spiritual preparation to survive, but in other areas we had to learn for ourselves. One huge area was management. When I achieved mainstream success, I was happy to turn over the financial daily details to someone else. This someone else was not only an accountant but a supersharp dealmaker. Sometimes dealmakers can be too sharp. When I got screwed over, Paul had the courtesy not to say, "I told you so," even though he had.

Paul was the first to tell me, "Hire Mark Rothbaum. He's not only tough but brilliant. He'll also take a bullet for you."

Mark became the man. And, not surprisingly, Mark's biggest protector became Paul. It began early on. Keep in mind that Mark, though confident, was a young man in his thirties. Youngest manager I'd ever hired.

We were playing an afternoon gig at Hughes Stadium in Sacramento. Waylon and Emmylou Harris were on the bill. Bill Graham was the promoter. Bill was already famous for being the roughest promoter in the business. Famous for throwing fits and even fists.

"Bill's one of my heroes," Mark told me. "It's going to be a thrill for me to meet him."

The thrill was short-lived. At the time, a group of Hells Angels were regulars at our shows. They liked our music and acted as volunteer security. But Bill didn't like the Hells Angels. They made him nervous.

"Get them the hell out of here," he told Mark.

"I can't," Mark answered.

"You better," Bill insisted.

"I won't." Mark was getting the idea. Mark wasn't about to be pushed around.

Once the show got started, things got heated. Mark had hired Showco, a Dallas firm, to set up the sound system. Bill thought the sound was lousy. We were about to start our set when we could hear Bill screaming at Mark, accusing him of incompetence and threatening not to pay us. The second Paul saw what was happening, he made a beeline for Bill, pulled out his pistol, and pointed it to Bill's head.

"This is our manager," Paul said, "and you will never, ever disrespect him."

"Put the gun away," Mark told Paul. "Bill just lost his temper."

I was interested to see how Bill, a supposed tough guy, would react.

"Bill's going to apologize, isn't he?" Paul asked as he inched closer to the promoter.

Feeling the cold metal against his temple, Bill said, "Yes, he is."

End of one story.

★

Beginning of another.

Paul had a friend from back in the day. Let's call him Shifty. Shifty was another Fort Worth gangster. Word was that Shifty had shot up a couple of state troopers and was on the run. Now the FBI wanted to run him down.

The FBI came calling just before a show in Nebraska. They cornered Mark.

"We need to talk to Willie's drummer," they demanded.

Mark did what any sane person would do. He went and found Paul.

"I hate to say this," Mark told Paul, "but the FBI is here. They want to talk to you."

Paul didn't blink. Not a single sign of apprehension.

"I'll clear out the dressing room and you can put them in there," Paul said.

The agents were seated in folding chairs when Paul made his appearance.

"We want to talk to you about Shifty," they said.

"Well, I'd like to kick your head in," Paul said.

"You can't talk to us like that," Agent One declared.

"I just did," Paul said.

"You're going to tell us about Shifty," Agent Two said.

"I'm telling you nothing."

Silence. Paul stared the agents dead in the eye.

The agents pounded him with questions.

"When did you first meet Shifty? When did you last see him? What's your connection to him?"

Paul's two-word answers never varied.

"Get lost."

The questions kept coming until Paul put them to a stop.

"Legally, I don't have to say anything. So, I'm thinking I was right all along. Rather than put up with your dumb questions, I'd do better to blast your brains out."

Sensing a force far greater than their own, the agents got out of there in a hurry.

★

Paul the Protector. Protecting Shifty from the FBI. Protecting Mark Rothbaum from Bill Graham. Protecting me from a slippery pattern, which usually had to do with women.

Easing into my forties, I still hadn't mastered the art of monogamy. No excuses. Just a plain fact. But, even admitting my weakness, I also have to say that many a time, I've been falsely accused. Doesn't matter whether it's a sawdust-on-the-floor beer hall or fancy concert hall; as a musician, I'm in a vulnerable position. Men can easily get the idea that I'm singing to their ladies. They think I'm flirting. Truth is, I'm not flirting. I'm just trying to stay in tune and maybe flirt with my muses. If girls are looking at me, well, there's nothing I can do about that.

I've lived through many such misunderstandings. A painful example: Phoenix, Arizona. Guy comes to my dressing room to say a bunch of folks are in the alley wanting my autograph. I don't think twice about it. Always been big on accommodating fans. Get to the alley, and, just like that, the guy goes after me with a crescent wrench. The blow lands, my head is cut, blood gushing everywhere. Incensed, I pick up a two-by-four and fight back like a tiger. Slam the board over his skull. But his skull is thicker than my board, and he doesn't go down. We go at it hard. He lands another blow to my shoulder. I get him across the cheek. We're so evenly matched I have no idea who'll be the last man standing. That is, until Paul pops up and, with a single punch to the guy's gut, knocks him to the ground. The dude's down for the count. Ambulance carts him off.

Later I learn that three months earlier, when I was in Phoenix, his wife went out with my band after the show. According to the boys, she just wanted to join them for a drink. All innocent fun. When she arrived home, though, she got to bragging about being with me. Understandably, her man marked his calendar for my return to town. His wife's fabrication resulted in seven stitches to my head.

Don't know how in hell Paul knew I was in peril. But it was a repeat performance of what had happened back in the day when I was still worked up on whiskey. Decades later, Paul's radar was sharper than ever. He never stopped tracking me.

HOLLYWOOD

1979 to 1986

"I'M NOT SURPRISED," Paul said when I was offered my first part in a film, *The Electric Horseman*.

I was extremely surprised. The film starred Robert Redford and Jane Fonda. The director was Sydney Pollack.

"You saw it coming?" I asked Paul.

"Hell yes. It happened to Crosby and Sinatra. So why not you? When you become a big enough singing star, they stick you in movies."

"Crosby and Sinatra had starring roles. I got a supporting role basically playing myself."

"Who better to play Willie Nelson? Besides, the roles are going to get better."

They did. A year later I had the lead in *Honeysuckle Rose* with Dyan Cannon and Amy Irving. Hollywood moves fast, and I had to learn to move with it. I was suddenly thrown into new situations and playing new venues.

HBO, for example, had come into its own as a major force. Every year they gave a big party in Hollywood for eight hundred prominent producers, directors, and actors. They asked me to entertain, and, given the $70,000 fee, I was inclined to accept.

The wingding took place in the fanciest hotel in Tinseltown. The media was out in force. Limos pulling up, paparazzi popping their bulbs, searchlights crisscrossing the sky, red carpet—the whole bit. Half an hour before we were about to go out and perform, Paul found the HBO suit in charge and said, "I'm Willie's money man. I'm here to get paid."

"No problem," the gentleman said. "I got a check right here."

"A check is a problem," Paul said. "Cash is not."

"Cash? Are you kidding?"

"Isn't Hollywood famous for pay for play? Well, we're playing for pay, and when it comes to payment, we are not playing around. Where I come from, cash is king."

"You go on in twenty-five minutes. How am I going to get seventy thousand dollars in twenty-five minutes?"

"You're asking the wrong guy."

"Look," the man insisted, "you're being unreasonable. Do you really think you're going to be stiffed? You're talking to HBO."

"You're talking to Paul English. And Paul English has learned that in this lifetime, you can get stiffed by anyone."

"I'm talking to Willie," the suit said.

"Won't do you any good," Paul said. "Willie's only going to tell you to talk to me. Which you already have. So, until I see a bag with seventy thousand dollars, you will not hear a lick of music."

Like so many Hollywood stories, this one had a happy ending. Only fifteen minutes after we were due onstage, someone showed up and handed Paul a tote bag stuffed with bills. He took his time counting it out.

"We're good to go on," he said. And so we did.

★

You'd think the Hollywood honchos would have learned their lesson, but the same scenario unfolded six months later in Tahoe. This time the stakes were even higher—a televised SHOWTIME special. SHOWTIME didn't impress Paul any more than HBO. He wanted cash on the barrelhead. They had a check. He said no.

"Time is money," the SHOWTIME exec said.

"Then you better hurry," Paul said.

This time they struck a compromise. A cashier's check. Paul was placated.

Paul was also pissed another time in Tahoe when he was too sick to make the gig and the promoters gave me a check. I put it in the back pocket of my jeans. Two days later, Paul came back and asked about it.

"Oh, dang it," I said, "I think I threw those jeans in the washer."

"I'm never letting you touch another check again," Paul said. Within an hour he convinced the casino to issue another payment.

★

Paul was a realist. Paul was practical. He found a way to merge practicality, loyalty, and love. Example: Luck, Texas.

The story started when I decided it was a good idea to turn "Red Headed Stranger," the song I'd sung to baby Lana when

I was deejaying in Fort Worth, into a full-tilt Hollywood movie.

"Why not bring Hollywood to Pedernales and shoot the film here?" Paul asked. He and his wife Janie, then pregnant with their son Paul Jr., had from time to time lived in my compound.

The thought of making a movie in my backyard had also occurred to me. Doesn't really take that much to read my mind since my mind isn't all that subtle, but Paul was the best at it. He knew what I wanted.

Problem was, Hollywood wasn't willing. They refused to finance the thing. I refused to give up. I turned to Don Tyson of the Tyson chicken empire. Don bought my vision. He put together an investor's package. I then got my buddy Bill Wittliff to pen the script, Morgan Fairchild to play my wife, and Katharine Ross to play the other woman. Even Paul himself, along with Bee Spears, had a role.

Principal photography was underway. We were already rolling when someone mentioned that we'd busted through the budget. But fortunate fate continued to befriend me in the form of my friend Carolyn Mugar. She and I, along with Neil Young and John Mellencamp, had started what would be the annual Farm Aid concerts benefiting the kind of working people I grew up with in Abbott. Carolyn was good enough to finance the completion of *Red Headed Stranger*, which, with the help of promoter/manager Shep Gordon, turned a profit for the investors.

To make the movie, we built a western town right there in Pedernales. I called it Luck. It was a typical cowboy set to look like the post–Civil War Wild West. Mostly facades of stores, stables, and a church. But we constructed a real-life saloon called World Headquarters. When filming was over, the question became: What do we do with Luck? I was fond of saying, "When you're here, you're in Luck. When you're not, you're out of Luck."

"So stay in Luck," Paul said.

"I intend to," I said. "But we could probably sell off this set to a studio for a pretty penny."

"Don't," Paul insisted. "It's too pretty to sell. Walking through it brings you pleasure. Besides, you can set up World Headquarters as your go-to dominoes and poker palace. You got all the Luck you need. Why change a thing?"

Paul was right. Come to Luck today, some thirty-seven years later, and you'll see that nothing has changed. World Headquarters is still there, and I'm still dealing.

Paul and Dan "Bee" Spears, the bass player that Paul and Willie "raised" (they found him when he was sixteen).

ON THE ROAD

Forever

PAUL WAS SITTING ACROSS FROM me on the bus. Between us was a table. On the table were spreadsheets listing all my accounts payable. He was scrutinizing these numbers like a biblical scholar studying the Dead Sea Scrolls. He did this for thirty minutes before stopping to pick up a novel.

"What are you reading?" I asked.

"James Fenimore Cooper. *The Last of the Mohicans*."

"Always meant to look at that. Is it good?"

"Great. The friendship between Natty Bumppo and his buddy Chingachgook reminds me of me and you."

"How?"

"They'd kill for each other. Like Ishmael and Queequeg in *Moby-Dick*."

"You've read *Moby-Dick*?"

"Twice. Cooper and Herman Melville are nineteenth-century novelists. Now I'm starting to read someone new."

"Who?"

"Someone who's gonna be bigger than Raymond Chandler. Mark my words." Paul had read every Raymond Chandler novel. Every Rex Stout novel. Every Ian Fleming.

"What's the book?" I asked.

"*A Time to Kill*."

"Who's the author?"

"John Grisham. The guy can write."

Paul became a John Grisham aficionado, reading every one of his novels the week it was published.

When it was time to go back to the spreadsheets, Paul found a minute error and corrected it. Then he moved from accounts payable to accounts receivable. I could hear him crunching those numbers in his head. Meanwhile, I was smoking a joint and thinking up a song about a guy with a head full of figures and a heart full of love.

Paul put down the paperwork and fished out a fat pile of *True Crime* magazines with headlines like "Woman Stuffs Fiancé and Hangs His Head on Wall" and "Eighty-Year-Old Bludgeons Twenty-One-Year-Old Lover with Tire Tool."

"Don't you get tired of reading those stories?" I asked.

"When I do, I go to the lighter stuff."

"Like what?"

"*True Detective*."

"Isn't it all the same?"

"No two stories are the same. That's why I can't stop reading them. One's crazier than the next."

"What about your own story?"

"You been hearing about it, Willie, since the day we met."

"Yeah, but it keeps getting better because you keep adding new details. There are always new twists and turns."

"That's why I keep reading. The more I read, the better my own story becomes."

"Why is that?"

"Because none of these stories are as good as mine."

The guys in the band, the fans we met along the road, the journalists who came to interview us—all of them agreed. They might listen to me for a minute or two, but if they were looking for real entertainment, they'd turn to Paul. Paul would mesmerize them. Paul would have them eating out of his hand. Paul would have you convinced that every word he said was true. Paul's stories satisfied eager listeners the way a good meal satisfies hungry diners. Two classic Paul examples:

PAUL STORY #1

We were on the bus, on our way to a gig in Chicago. Paul and Bee were watching *Wheel of Fortune*, their favorite TV show. They loved Vanna White.

"Look what she's wearing today," Bee said.

"It's even better than what she had on yesterday," Paul declared.

When the show finished, we were all sitting around: me, Bee, Mickey, Paul's brother Billy, who'd also been playing drums for us for a good spell, guitarist Grady Martin, and manager Mark Rothbaum. It was thundering outside. Rain coming down like it was the last days. We had time to kill, and Paul had stories to tell.

"I know I've told y'all about the Peroxide Boys."

"You have," Mickey said, "but tell us again."

"You haven't heard this story," Paul said, "because I've been saving it for a rainy day like this. Well, sir, of all the Peroxide Boys, I was the most peroxided. My hair was the color of golden wheat. Of all the Peroxide Boys, I was also the ballsiest. When things got nasty, the boys turned to me.

I'm talking about the time when Frank the Finger got stung. We called him the Finger not because he'd shoot you the shaft but because he was our best shot. His trigger finger was always itching. One night at a Jacksboro Highway joint, it got to itching too much. He thought this ole boy was making a pass at his girl. Wasn't all that easy for the Finger to get him a girl.

"I say that because, despite his highly developed skill with a forty-five, he was not the prettiest Peroxide Boy. His teeth needed fixing, the peroxide had his hair going off in six different directions, and his nose looked like a light bulb. You can understand that once he had finally wooed and won a gal, he was dead set on keeping her. 'Stay the hell away,' he told this fella who took one look at the Finger and sorely underestimated him. Fella put his arm around the Finger's gal and started waltzing her to the dance floor but never made it there. That's because the Finger shot him in the kneecap. I knew the story wouldn't end there since this fella had friends—bikers called the Road Killers—who swore to get even.

"A couple of weeks passed before the Finger went out to his mailbox. Reached his hand inside. A rattlesnake snapped into action and bit down into the Finger's finger. The Finger fell out. His gal rushed him to the hospital; it was a close call, but they got the venom out in time. He was too shook up to go into payback mode. As Revenger in Chief, the task fell to me.

"I took my time. I knew my adversaries expected an instant reaction, which was why I did the opposite. I waited a full year because I figured by then they'd be sure they had scared us off. They had stopped looking over their shoulders.

"It was late August when I made my move. The Road Killers were setting off on a midnight picnic over at Bachman

Lake in Dallas, a woodsy little hideaway on the north side of Love Field. They took over the place. Them and their gals got sloppy drunk. Popped pills. Partied so hard they were jumping nude into the lake.

"All the while I was watching. All the while I was with my buddy Mike, a guy I grew up with. Mike worked over at the Dallas Zoo in Oak Cliff. His job was to feed the reptiles. Mike knew his snakes. Mike knew where to get me a half dozen rattlers. Mike was willing to accept a generous payment and accompany me, along with his bagful of hungry snakes, over to Bachman. While the blissed-out Road Killers were busy splashing around, Mike put a hungry rattler in each of the motorcycle boots the boys had taken off before running into the lake. Mike also constructed a thin but strong netting to insert inside the boots so the snakes couldn't crawl out.

"We waited and watched from a safe distance until the Road Killers got out of the water, dried themselves off, and started getting dressed. As they stepped into the boots, the stuff hit the fan. I wish you could have been there. It was epic. It was beautiful. The Road Killers were running around like roaches. The Road Killers were crying for their mammas. Their girlfriends didn't know what to do while their Road Killers were throwing their boots into the lake and screaming to the heavens for divine intervention. But the good Lord did not interfere. Justice was served. I went home a happy man."

PAUL STORY #2

Another *Honeysuckle Rose* bus ride.

"Have I told y'all about Kicks Cartwheel?" he asked.

If he had told us, we wanted to hear it again.

Every time Paul told the story, he told it differently.

"Kicks Cartwheel was a rodeo clown. Well, Fort Worth was a great rodeo town. I got a special kick out of Kicks because I'd known him since grade school. Funny little guy who the big boys liked to pick on. Except I wouldn't let them. Kicks had a sweet disposition and wouldn't hurt a fly. But his floppy feet and elephant ears made him a target. While he was in school, I made sure no one messed with him, but then he went out in the world where he had a tough time. The army rejected him cause he wore Coke-bottle eyeglasses and was half blind. For a while he worked as a postman but kept getting lost on his route. He pumped gas, he drove a dump truck, he slabbed on drywall. Poor Kicks tried everything, but nothing clicked until he got this idea of wearing a clown's outfit and entertaining at parties. He found his calling. One thing led to another. His big break came when a traveling rodeo took him on. He played the circuit. He made kids laugh.

"When he came with the rodeo to Fort Worth for the first time, two of our old schoolmates showed up. Naturally they were drunk as skunks, and, as Kicks was running around the arena, they tripped him and pulled off his polka-dot pants. He was standing there in just his Fruit of the Looms. Everyone thought it was funny except for me. I threw him a big towel so he could cover up. It took me a few minutes to figure out my next move, but when I did, I knew it was the right one.

"I joined up with our old schoolmates and pretended to approve of their stunt. 'You guys are hysterical,' I said. 'Pass me a beer.' I didn't drink the beer. I didn't do anything but wait until the bull rider got ready to do his thing. Just before they opened the gate and let the bull and his rider bust out, I punched out both our old schoolmates who were too wasted to put up a fight. Then I did more than pull off their jeans. I also pulled off their Fruit of the Looms and threw them out there with the bull. By then the bull had dislodged the rider and went for Kicks's tormentors. Balls out, butt naked except for their T-shirts, these two swinging dicks ran for their lives. The bull got corralled, but I was careful to close all the gates so the crowd could have a good long look at the guys trying to cover up hairy crotches with the palms of their hands."

After hearing the story, I asked Paul, "Is that true?"

He was laughing too hard to answer.

OUR LIFE AS A MOVIE

A Strange and Cinematic Time

NOT ONLY WAS PAUL AROUND when I started making movies, he appeared in some of those movies himself, like *Honeysuckle Rose*, *Songwriter*, and *Red Headed Stranger*. Most people would have been just a little intimidated in the presence of Robert Redford or Jane Fonda or Dyan Cannon. Not Paul. Paul moved right in the middle of the mix and started telling stories to these Hollywood stars like they were his best friends. They loved him.

Paul also wasn't shy about coming up with movie ideas of his own. He once took a writer aside and laid out a grand plan.

"You know the song 'Me and Paul'?" he asked.

"Sure. Everyone knows 'Me and Paul.'"

"Well, I got a story to go with it."

"Isn't the song already a story?" the writer asked.

"It's the start of a story. A story that lasts four minutes. My story lasts two hours. It makes for a great movie script. Want to hear it?"

"Do I have a choice?"

"No. Just sit back and listen. We start off in Abbott, Texas. That's where Willie was born. But this Willie is different from the real Willie. This Willie has a superpower. Every time he picks up a guitar, he's like Popeye downing a can of spinach. He can take on a dozen guys twice his size and turns them to mincemeat. The guitar has a name—Trigger. It isn't a fancy guitar. It's beat up but beautiful. It contains Willie's soul.

"While Willie is coming of age in Abbott, you got his sidekick, Paul English, kicking up dust in Fort Worth. Paul has a superpower as well. He can see the past, and he can also see the future. He knows what's gonna happen before it happens. What do you think so far?"

"So far so good," the writer said.

"Hang on. I'm just getting started. Every story has to have a villain, right?"

"Right."

"My story has two villains. One's a man named Reno. The other's a woman named Vera Lou. They both want to take Willie down."

"Why?"

"Because Willie represents good and they represent evil. Every story is a fight between good and evil. That's a given. No tension, no drama. So Willie's dramatic struggle is holding on to his guitar. Without it, he's through. And naturally Reno and Vera Lou are going to do all they can to get the guitar out of my man's hands. Reno does it by luring Willie into high-stakes poker games. Willie can't resist a good poker game. And Vera Lou's way of seducing is no different than the way Cleopatra landed Julius Caesar. I don't have to spell that out for you, do I?"

"I get it," the writer said.

"So will the movie fans," Paul said. "They'll understand why Willie puts his guitar to the side when Reno comes over with his poker chips and band of card sharks. They'll also understand why, when Vera Lou weaves her sensuous spell over him, he can't be all that worried about Trigger. No red-blooded man, no matter his dedication to the straight and narrow, can resist Vera Lou. Vera Lou makes Marilyn Monroe look like Mary Poppins.

"Every movie—for that matter, every story—has three acts, three parts. Beginning, middle, and end. Act one: Reno runs off with Trigger while Willie's all engrossed in a night of fiery five-card stud. He's winning, he's losing, he's winning again. But when the night is over and Willie decides to do a little picking to help him fall asleep, he reaches for his guitar case. It's empty. No Trigger. No worries. Paul's on the case. Paul's perceptive powers see that Reno is about to sell Trigger to a young buck out looking to replace Willie as king of country music. He wants Trigger's superpower for himself. Young Buck and Reno are set to meet at a crossroads on a muddy highway. Instead of meeting the young buck, though, Reno meets me. Before he knows what hits him, I send him reeling and send Trigger back to his beloved owner.

"Act two: Vera Lou is slicker than Reno. Poker is powerful, but nothing is more powerful than a gorgeous gal, especially one with curves like Vera Lou. Vera Lou has a plan that will let her get to Willie and, in the aftermath, run off with Trigger. She'll tire him out in bed, and then, when he's sleeping, she'll go creeping off in the night with Trigger under her arm. It's a devious plan, and the only way to derail it is stop it before it happens. It happens at a show in Oklahoma. Vera Lou has found a place just in front of the stage. Her outfit is outrageous. She's wiggling and waving and displaying her goods in ways that cannot be ignored. Willie is looking. Willie is wanting. Willie is willing. But because I foresee the future, I derail Vera Lou's devious plot. Appropriately enough, the last song of the night is 'Amazing Grace.' After the last grace note of the amazing song, I stand up from behind my drum kit and shout out, 'Terrorist alert!' No one's allowed backstage. I escort Willie to the bus, and just like that, we're whisked away. Vera Lou kicks the stage and curses my name.

"Act three: The climax. The most exciting act of all. Reno and Vera Lou decide to combine forces with the devil. It's the devil who wants to take down Willie, the devil who wants to gut that guitar and strip Willie of his superpower to touch people's hearts with kindness and love. The devil, being the fallen angel and cleverest con man in the cosmos, knows that to get to Willie he's got to get to me. Because I wear the costume of the devil—that's my act, that's my image—the devil reasons that if he can replace me, he can remove the one guy standing between him and Willie. Rather than replace me, the devil figures he can become me. He can make Willie think he, the devil, is me, Paul. So, eliminate Paul, put on Paul's outfit, and let Reno and Vera Lou do their thing. Combine a night of poker with a night of lovemaking. Slip in and slip out with Trigger. Make a bonfire and toast Trigger like a marshmallow. Watch the wood turn to ashes. Celebrate the victory of evil over good.

"The plan almost works. It almost works because while my superpower allows me to see in advance the plans of human beings, the devil is not human.

"On a Saturday night in Dallas, with a gig only hours away, the devil gives me a bad case of the flu. My brother Billy plays drums with Willie as well. So, Willie's covered, but I want to call him and tell him I'm sick. That's when the devil zaps my phone. I got no service. I'm laid up in bed. Meanwhile, the devil shows up as me. Takes on my face. My figure. My voice. And, of course, puts on my black cape. Naturally no one notices. Not even brother Billy. Devil can fool anyone. The show goes on. Devil plays drums like me. Willie's feeling that something's a little different with the beat, but it's not different enough to make him question me. He thinks Paul's just having an off night.

"Night is over. Show is done. Talking as me, the devil says to Willie, 'Couple of friends are having a card game right down the street. They're dying to meet you.'

"Willie says, 'Never known you to push me to play poker with strangers, Paul.'

"'Well, Willie,' says the Devil Pretending to be Paul, 'these folks are no strangers. They're some of my best friends. Good people. Go on down there. I guarantee that you'll have fun. This here boy, Reno, I been knowing before I met you back in in Fort Worth. This gal, Vera Lou, used to deal in Vegas, didn't you, darling?' Vera Lou, standing right there, nods yes. She's wearing a peekaboo blouse with the buttons about to pop and a supertight shiny gold leotard.

"'Meet Reno," Devil Paul says. 'He's as honest as the day is long. And be sure and bring Trigger along, Willie. These folks might inspire you to work on a song, that's how much fun they are.'

"'Well, Paul, if you say so.' Devil Paul says so. Reno, Vera Lou, and Willie—with Trigger in hand—are off to play cards at an undisclosed location.

"Me, the real me, is having convulsions. I'm in bed with the sweats. I'm feverish. I'm hallucinating. I know something's not right. I'm tossing and turning until I'm falling out of the bed. Back in the bed, I get the shivers all over again. My hands are shaking, my legs are twitching, until I'm finally exhausted enough to fall into a sleep where I'm dreaming a dream so vivid I'm sure it's real. I'm seeing numbers. I'm seeing red letters. Number 8. Number 4. Number 8. 848, flashing on and off one of those monster-sized neon signs in Times Square. 848. 848. 848. Then I start seeing letters. A. K. A. R. D. Over and over again. AKARD. Those letters, like the numbers, are also flashing in bloodred neon. 848 Akard. That's it! That's the address. That's God—or some angel, or whatever forces of good are operating inside me—telling me to get over to 848 Akard Street. Doesn't matter that I got a fever. Doesn't matter that I'm sweating like a hog. I jump out of bed, throw on clothes, grab my cape, and race down to 848 Akard.

"Can this be the place? Looks like some kind of warehouse. Do I have it right? I know I do when I see myself standing in front of the door. Devil Paul is blocking the entrance. Well, Devil Paul is no match for Real Paul. I bust out of the car and get up in his face. I'm facing my own face.

"'You ain't me,' I say. 'You ain't nothing but a fake.'

"'You've been disguising yourself as me for years,' he says. 'You been stealing my thunder, so now I'm stealing yours. Get the hell out of here.'

"'You're already in hell,' I tell the devil. 'You're hell itself, and hell doesn't scare me.'

"'You don't have the balls to take me on,' Devil Paul says.

"'If you have any balls at all, kiss them goodbye,' I say as I kick him in the nuts.

"I can't testify that the devil has testicles. All I can say is that one vicious kick does bring him down. He collapses. I pick him up and throw him in a nearby garbage dumpster before going into the warehouse where Willie and Reno are playing poker. Willie's got all the chips. 'Having a good night, Paul,' he says.

"'Where's Trigger?' I ask.

"'Right in the corner,' Willie says. But we look in the corner, and there's nothing but an empty chair.

"'Where's Vera Lou?' I ask.

"'Didn't you see her leave?' Reno asks, thinking I'm Devil Paul. 'She went to the store to get us something to eat.' I rush out just as Vera Lou is pulling in. She's driving a gold Caddy. She's wearing gold earrings, that bosom-busting blouse, and that skintight gold leotard. She gets out of the car with a bag of burgers. She looks at me and gives me a thumbs-up. She thinks I'm Devil Paul.

"'You take care of Trigger?' I ask.

"'Trigger's safe and sound,' she answers.

"'What'd you do with him?'

"'Just what you asked me to do.'

"Now *I* don't know what to do. I can't let anyone know that Devil Paul is out cold and Real Paul is out to save the day. I let Vera Lou bring in the burgers while I go back to the dumpster. I pull out Devil Paul and slap him around until he comes to.

"'It's me and you,' I say.

"'We're the same. You don't want to believe it, but we are.'

"'Might be the same coin, but we got different sides.'

"'I got Willie's heart," the devil says. 'I got Willie's soul. I got Trigger. And ain't nothing you can do to change that. You see, son, you got here too late. You're way behind the beat.'

"I say, 'Willie plays behind the beat. Willie sings behind the beat. You don't understand that. You don't understand his heart. You don't understand his soul.'

"'I'm a better timekeeper than you'll ever be,' he says. 'I'm the real deal.'

"'You're as fake as a pair of falsies.'

"'Say what you want, drummer. I already got what I came for.'

"At just about that time, Reno, Vera Lou, and Willie step outside to see Devil Paul and me facing each other. Reno and Vera Lou are flabbergasted.

"'There's two devils,' Reno says. 'How we gonna know which one is real?'

"'I don't believe in the devil,' Willie says. 'Never have and never will. I just believe in goodness. Positive energy. Positive thinking. The devil is just a figment of man's imagination. He doesn't exist.'

"And with that, Devil Paul, in a puff of smoke, evaporates into thin air.

"'Well, Paul,' Willie says, 'now that I made off with a devil's worth of winnings, let's go down the street to that all-night pawn shop and pick up Trigger. I can hear him calling to me.'"

Having reached the end of his story, Paul asked the writer, who'd been taking down his every word, "What do you think?"

The writer paused for a bit, looked at Paul, and said, "I don't think I'll be playing poker with Willie Nelson anytime soon."

A PLACE TO FORGET

A Time to Forget

FOR TOO LONG TO REMEMBER, I had an epic battle with the IRS over a supposed $32 million in back taxes. The thing went on for years. Just like that, they took everything I owned, houses and ranches, buses and trucks and recording studios. The press wrote me off. Said I was through.

"Heroes are never through," Paul said. "You'll find a way. The bigger the obstacle, the stronger you get."

I felt like Paul was talking more about himself than about me. As it turned out, though, Paul's optimism proved true. Mark Rothbaum put together a legal team that took on the IRS. Mark came up with a winning strategy.

In a conversation with Paul, I found a way to supplement that strategy.

"You've always found a way to make money making music," Paul said. "Here's another chance."

I took a chance on making a record where the proceeds would go to the IRS—*The IRS Tapes: Who'll Buy My Memories?*

The IRS bought the idea and so did the public.

The crisis passed. When solvency returned and the story ended triumphantly, Paul said, "Now you're more a hero than ever."

In truth, I saw Paul as a hero. I believed he'd earned that designation. If you want to get fancy, you could call him an antihero. I suppose antiheroes can be seen as bad guys who, because they're charming, win us over. But I don't really think there was anything bad about Paul. He was, in fact, a true hero.

Bee Spears, our bass player, liked to tell the story about the time he and Paul were leaving a motel in Las Cruces, New Mexico, to drive to our gig. In walking to the bus, they passed by the motel pool. Paul was in full regalia—black cape, boots, hat, the whole nine yards. He glanced over and saw a woman by the pool with her head buried in a magazine. Her infant crawled to the water's edge and fell in. The mother didn't notice. Paul did and, without a moment's thought, leaped into the pool, grabbed the child, and brought the infant to the surface. Dripping wet, child in his arms, he walked over to the shocked, negligent mother, and handed her the infant. The mother's eyes turned red.

"Give me my baby!" she screamed, as though Paul, instead of saving the child, had tried to kidnap her.

Bee wondered what Paul would do. Paul was soaked to the bone. He had performed an act of heroism and, in turn, was greeted with scorn. Would he give this woman a piece of his mind? Would he tell her that if she had been watching her child, this never would have happened? Would he put her in her place?

"None of that," Bee said. "Paul just walked back to his room, took a quick shower, and put on an outfit just like the one that got soaking wet. I asked him if he was pissed. 'No,' he said. 'The woman was scared that her baby had almost drowned. So, she took her fear out on me. That's fine. No harm done. Let's go make some music.'"

★

Another time we were in Bakersfield, California. Poodie Locke, our road manager for over thirty years, was with Paul after the show. Stomping grounds of my lifelong buddy Merle Haggard, Bakersfield wasn't exactly the Garden of Eden. Bakersfield was a tough town. Poodie and Paul were heading toward the bus when a pretty teenage girl hurriedly walked past. On her heels was a guy, somewhere in his thirties, screaming obscenities about the young lady's anatomy. When he actually reached out and grabbed her rear end, Paul snapped.

"He got up in the dude's face," Poodie said, "and told him to leave the lady alone."

"Who the hell are you?" the predator asked, looking over Paul's getup. "The devil at some Halloween party?"

Paul didn't bother to reply. He just whipped out his pistol.

The guy froze before fainting. The girl thanked Paul and walked away.

When they got to the bus and Poodie told us the story, Paul played it down. All he said was "The devil's gotta do what the devil's gotta do."

★

Another Poodie/Paul story: They found themselves in the big post office in downtown Denver. It was a week before Christmas, and they were mailing gift packages to friends and family around the country. The line was long. The heating system had broken down, and it was cold as hell. Everyone was impatient. Everyone was looking to get up to the window, do their business, and get out. After nearly an hour, Poodie and Paul were second in line. They saw that the man at the window was having a hard time telling the postal worker what he wanted. He had a severe stutter.

The longer it took, the angrier everyone behind this guy became. Everyone could hear him trying to get the words out.

"Hey, Porky Pig," some redneck in line said, "if you can't get the goddamn words out, move out of the way."

That made the man even more nervous. He stuttered even more. Other people in the line, more impatient than ever, picked up on what the redneck had said.

"Porky Pig," the tormentor repeated, and suddenly everyone started chanting, "Porky Pig, Porky Pig, Porky Pig, Porky Pig . . ."

That's when Paul turned around and faced everyone behind him.

"If you d-d-d-d-don't w-w-w-w-w-want your pig p-p-p-porked," he said, pretending that he, too, had a stutter, "you'd better s-s-s-s-shut the hell up."

Seeing the fury in Paul's eyes, the tormentors stopped tormenting. Only the redneck came up face-to-face with Paul.

"Who you calling a p-p-p-p-pig?" Paul asked the dude.

Wisely, the dude didn't answer. He walked away.

★

I consider anyone who keeps me out of a jail a hero. Paul did it twice (at least). First time was in Laredo, the Texas city north of the Rio Grande. After a gig, Paul and I crossed the border to Nuevo Laredo to check out the red-light district. When we returned to the motel, we didn't get past the manager's office. A cop stopped me and showed me a half-smoked joint a maid had found in my room. This was back when a half-smoked joint meant jail time. Paul saw what was happening and kept walking like he didn't know me. While I was trying to smooth talk the officer, Paul got to my room, took the big stash of weed from my guitar case, and flushed it down the toilet. When he returned to the lobby, he acted surprised to see me.

"What's happening here, Willie?" he asked.

"This police officer says they found a joint in my room."

"Must have been the joint the mayor's son was smoking and forgot to take with him."

"The mayor's son?" the cop asked.

"The mayor's son is a big Willie Nelson fan. So is the mayor. They were both at the show last night. Next time we come through, we'd like you to come to the show as our honored guest."

Case closed.

Another case opened in El Paso when, unbeknownst to us, the city was going through a crackdown on anything illicit. Paul got wind of the fact that the cops were heading for our bus with drug-sniffing dogs. There was a whole lot of potent weed on board. No time to dump it. In the nick of time, Paul spotted a burger joint across the street. He ran over and returned with two dozen greasy chili cheeseburgers hot off the grill and a pound of greasy chili cheese fries. When the dogs arrived, they went right for the meat. Paul was kind enough to save enough burgers and fries so the police officers could enjoy their lunch.

PORTRAIT OF PAUL AS AN ARTIST

Night and Day

IT WAS A MOODY NIGHT in Missouri. We'd played Saint Louis, and we'd be playing Louisville the next day. We were up and excited. We'd just put on a good show, and the crowd had given us big love. I wanted to play poker. Paul wanted to draw.

Paul loved to draw. I already told you about his talent for bowling and leather tooling, but sketching was a different deal entirely. Paul was a great sketcher. Sketching was part of his imagination. Part of his story. But rather than me telling that story, I'm going to let Paul explain his pictures.

WOMAN NEXT TO "HELP KEEP OUR CITY CLEAN" TRASH CAN

"Takes me back to my childhood in Fort Worth. I'd see these luscious ladies of the night. Lots of folks considered them

trash. I didn't. I liked looking at them. I thought they had strength and style. I tried to draw them with dignity. I put in the trash can to show the hypocrisy of the local government looking to keep the city 'clean.' To them, clean meant no sex. To me, sex—and especially sexy women—were beautiful."

WOMAN SEATED NEXT TO COLUMN

"His full name was Joaquin Alberto Vargas y Chávez, but, for short, he went by Vargas. He came from Peru. In 1919 he started drawing girls in the Ziegfeld Follies. During World War II, he created the Vargas Girl pinups. He worked for

Esquire and then got even more famous in 1959 when Hugh Hefner started using his sketches in *Playboy*. Vargas was my man. Don't get me wrong. I appreciate Picasso. I appreciate Salvador Dalí. I appreciate all the masters like Monet and Van Gogh. I even liked it when Andy Warhol started painting soup cans. Pop art was fun. But pinup art—man, that's what called to me. Peekaboo art. Show the lady but leave room for the imagination. Show her see-through top. Show her flirty smile. Her pretty hair. Her 'I'm all yours' attitude. Show how she loves being shown."

MARILYN MONROE

"Count me among the millions of men who saw her as the sexiest siren in history. I know enough Greek mythology to tell you that the original sirens were half women, half birds who made sailors crazy with their sweet songs. Even though I devoured Rex Stout and Mickey Spillane murder mysteries, I once read Homer's *Odyssey* and remembered that Odysseus, the hero, made his men stick wax in their ears so they wouldn't hear the siren's song. When Marilyn sang 'Happy Birthday, Mr. President' to JFK, I do not believe he had wax in his ears. No man could resist her. This drawing is only one of many that I made of her. I drew this one after seeing her in *The Seven Year Itch.* Or maybe it was *Some Like It Hot.* Anyway, she had her own brand of heat. It was a whisper-quiet smoldering heat that, as far as I'm concerned, will never grow cold or old."

MR. PERFECT

"As a kid in Fort Worth, I used to wander over to the local library. I loved looking through the art books. One of the things I remember most was a book of sketches by Michelangelo. He loved drawing men with perfect physiques. That gave me the idea of drawing a guy I called Mr. Perfect. I see him as a combination muscle man and wrestler. I gave him an attitude that says, 'I've done it. I've achieved the body of life.' If you look closely, though, you'll see that his fingers are a little feminine. I did that in order to say, 'No matter how manly we might be, there's a touch of femininity in every man, whether he admits it or not.'"

EMPTY ROOM WITH UPHOLSTERED CHAIRS AND COFFEE TABLE

"In another lifetime, I might have been an interior decorator. That's why I drew up this room. Everything matches. The floral figures on the sides of the easy chair match the two lampshades. You'll notice on the coffee table there's a book of clams. That's because I like drawing shellfish. I like designing a perfectly proportioned, calm and inviting living room. The room represents the domestic peace and happiness that I found with my wife Janie. Everything is in order. The craziness of my old ways is behind me. There's a fireplace. There's serenity. Thanks to Janie, life finally makes sense. I can calm down, sit in one of those chairs, pick up my sketchpad, and write this poem:

Well, I've been up, I've been down
Some say I've been around
Fast cars, easy living, easy going
Never giving, never a frown
Playing music from town to town
Thought life had gone and wanted to lay it down
Then from the blue someone said,
'Paul, this is Janie, she'd like to meet you'
Well, now I'm running ahead of the pack
Looking up, never back
My head is high, my feet are on the ground
My past is gone, life is found
For I have Janie, the sweetest gal in any town

Love, Paul."

HARSH REALITY

2010

"THIS STROKE'S A JOKE." That's the first thing Paul said to me when I saw him in the hospital. He was seventy-seven and, until then, showed no signs of slowing down. If anyone seemed indestructible, it was Paul.

His brother Billy, our number two drummer, and Paul's wife Janie have told me what happened before and after the stroke.

"We were riding the bus from Austin to Virginia. Paul was showing some symptoms. I knew he wasn't right. He knew he wasn't right, but he wasn't about to cancel the trip.

"'We need to get to a hospital, Paul,' I said.

"He said, 'We don't need to do anything but get to the gig.' I knew my brother well enough not to argue, but anyone could see something was wrong."

"They called me from the bus and put Paul on," Janie said. "'It's nothing but the flu,' he said. I could hear in his voice that it was much more than the flu. I told Billy to get him to the nearest hospital. As it turned out, the West Virginia University

Health System actually has a renowned stroke facility. The doctors' diagnosis didn't take long. My husband had suffered a stroke."

"His mobility was still good," Billy said, "but his speech was not. He'd been a whiz at the computer, and, unfortunately, those skills were gone. At the same time, his spirit never sagged."

"When he got back to Dallas," Janie said, "he was doing those sudoku puzzles as easily as ever. Paul was the king of sudoku. Stroke or no stroke, his mind was still clicking on all cylinders."

That spring we were set to tour Europe.

"Paul," I said, "you better stay home with Janie and rest up a bit."

"Are you kidding, Willie? When have I ever been any good at resting up? Resting up would bring on another stroke. I'm going to Europe."

There was no changing his mind.

In Europe, Billy took over more of the drum duties, yet Paul, dressed in his black hat and cape, was onstage every night keeping time.

"This devil is not going away anytime soon," he said.

There were a few scary moments when we thought he had gone away. In Amsterdam, just before showtime, he wandered off, and no one could find him. Never had happened before. Paul was Mr. Punctuality. We panicked. Called the police. Went on a search mission ourselves, calling out his name in a city that none of us knew. Had he fallen into one of the canals? Had he lost himself in one of those souvenir shops? We were scared to death. Where the hell was Paul?

"Where the hell do you think I'd be?" he asked when we returned to the hotel and saw him seated calmly in the lobby.

"You weren't here before," his brother Billy said.

"Well, I'm here now. Let's get rolling."

I never did learn where he'd wandered off to, and because I was so happy to see him safe, I never did ask.

The wonderful thing was that every single night, despite his physical impairment, he never failed to flash his million-dollar smile. We never heard him complain. Post-stroke, he seemed as joyful as pre-stroke. So, when he kept saying, "This stroke's a joke," I tended to believe him.

★

The stroke turned out to be the first physical challenge. The second, three years later, happened just when I thought Paul had refound his footing.

November 23, 2013.

Billy was there. Here's his firsthand account:

"After a gig at WinStar World Casino in Oklahoma just over the Texas border, we headed out on the bus. Everyone was sleeping when *boom!* The bus crashed into a bridge. I was in a lower bunk, and, after being jostled around like a little doll, I felt the upper bunk collapse on me. I immediately thought of my brother Paul who was in the horseshoe-shaped bedroom in the back, but I couldn't get to him. Someone yelled, 'Fire!' I thought the bus was about blow. I still couldn't move. Our security guard managed get to me out. I reached in the closet and grabbed Trigger, Willie's guitar, which miraculously hadn't been hurt. I do believe God watches over that guitar. I still didn't know where Paul was. Turned out they had to cut through metal to free him from the back bedroom where he was trapped. He and I rode in the ambulance together. He was breathing—he was alive!—but he was hurt a lot worse than me. On impact, the heavy safe in his back bedroom came flying out and landed on his feet. His feet were smashed and covered in blood."

As his wife Janie remembers:

"His foot was broken, and the tendons in his ankle were severed. The big blow, though, was the concussion. He didn't realize it at first, but the doctors confirmed it. From the moment he woke up from surgery, he tried speaking but was impeded by a severe stutter. The more he tried, the more frustrated he became. Over time, the stutter intensified to where he wouldn't speak at all. Paul English, the world's greatest storyteller, was reduced to silence."

When you part from your friend, you grieve not;
For that which you love most in him may be clearer in his absence, as the mountain to the climber is clearer from the plain. And let there be no purpose in friendship save the deepening of the spirit.

KAHLIL GIBRAN,
The Prophet

Paul with his three sons: Evan (left) in the Duke T-shirt, Darrell, and Paul Jr. (right).

The family at Evan's wedding just a few months before Paul's death.
PHOTO BY EMILY CHAPPELL

THE QUIET YEARS

The Recent Past

THERE'S STRENGTH IN SILENCE.

That's an accurate description of Paul's last years. They were beautifully silent. Paul's silence only added to his authority, dignity, and stature. He never lost his spirit. And—if you can believe it—despite the stroke and the concussion he suffered from the accident, he never stopped touring with us. *Ever.*

He hung in. He soldiered on. The enormous physical challenges never broke him. He remained the tough son of a bitch he'd always been. He remained the heart and soul of the Family. I was certain that nothing would take my brother down.

And yet, fate gets even the best of us. When I look back, I do find truth in the philosophy that we are one another's angels and demons. Paul was my angel, and life was our church. And my wish is that in carving out this long and winding story for you, dear reader, we are becoming Paul's angels, too, singing his name to our loved ones at home or silently to ourselves.

"When he was off the road with Willie and came home to Dallas," Janie said, "he was a loving husband, father, and grandad. His grandson, Trey, was the apple of his eye. And even though Paul couldn't speak, he communicated with Trey through drawing. He'd draw elephants and clowns and dinosaurs and gorillas. He'd wear crazy hats and put on silly glasses that would make Trey howl with delight. He devoted his time and loving attention to his sons, Darrell Wayne, Paul Jr., and Evan. And then, of course, there were his dogs. He adored his dogs. Bamba, a catlike mutt. Tico, a Havanese named after his friend Tico Torres, Jon Bon Jovi's drummer. Then there were our big two strays, Buck and Django, who slept in our bed. When the holidays came around, Paul sprang into action. He became Chevy Chase's Clark Griswold in *National Lampoon's Christmas Vacation.* Had to have the biggest tree. Had to have the most fabulous outdoor lighting in the neighborhood. Up on that ladder, he had to do it all by himself.

"During the day, he listened to music nonstop. Mainly Willie's music. He never missed an episode of *Wheel of Fortune.* He loved going to the Dallas Summer Musicals where we had season tickets. In earlier days, we had seen Lena Horne's one-woman show. Paul had taken Paul Jr. to see *Tommy* with Roger Daltrey. His interest in movies never waned. He loved comedies, loved Denzel Washington action films, loved murder mysteries where, annoyingly, he'd figure out who had done it—and have to tell me—before the story was half over.

"He never abandoned his trusty trumpet. People forget that Paul played trumpet before he took up drums. When the boys were small, he'd wake them up every morning by blasting Pérez Prado's 'Cherry Pink and Apple Blossom White.' Every morning, I still hear that melody in my mind. That melody contained so much of Paul's sweetness."

★

After the Christmas holidays in 2019, we were back on the road, and Paul was still with us. In January we were playing San Francisco when Paul complained of stomach pain. Remember—Paul never complained, so I knew something had to be wrong. He flew home to Janie who checked him into the hospital.

"After a battery of tests and every sort of endoscopy," Janie said, "they concluded that he had a blockage in his mesenteric artery. They put in a stent. After the procedure, Paul came out of it feeling awesome. That was Paul. He was going to prevail no matter what. He was given a walker, but he used it as a snare, beating out rhythms with this drumsticks on the bar connecting the aluminum legs. Keeping time, always keeping time. 'Time is on my side,' he liked to say. He was getting better, stronger, even more determined. He came home renewed and reenergized. I couldn't help but be hopeful. Hope didn't last long. He took a sudden downward turn and was back in the hospital. Doctors feared it was pneumonia. There was also internal bleeding from the stent. I called everyone to the hospital. Darrell Wayne drove up. RP and Evan were with him as well. We had a good day. Paul was smiling and listening to our chatter. For hours, I held his hand. Then suddenly the monitors went crazy, and the nurses made us leave. It was code blue. It was the end. Paul passed February 11, 2020."

★

Forgive me—I'm not good at eulogies. When I love someone like I loved Paul, words stop working. All I can say is that I'm eternally grateful for a friendship that endured and strengthened over sixty-five years. Never an argument. Never a misunderstanding. Nothing but unbreakable, undying trust. I can't tell you how many times, after hearing the news, I thought to myself: *I need to talk to Paul; I need him next to me; I need his advice; I need to feel his presence; I need his love.*

The headline in the *Washington Post* read, "Paul English, Willie Nelson's Best Friend, Drummer and Formidable Enforcer, Dies at 87."[8]

That was the short version.

A longer—and a deeply touching—version was given by Janie at Paul's homecoming celebration, held, appropriately enough, at Billy Bob's Texas nightclub in the Fort Worth Stockyards. I want Janie to have the last word.

"Of course, there was music," she remembered. "As much as Paul loved Willie, he also loved Ray Wylie Hubbard. He once told me, 'I want that kid to sing at my funeral.' So he did. He sang 'I Still Can't Believe You're Gone,' invoking the precious memory of Carlene. And, of course, he sang, 'Me and Paul.' Ray Benson from Asleep at the Wheel sang as well. Mickey Raphael spoke. My boys spoke. I spoke about how delighted Paul was when Willie's children, Paula and Amy and Lukas and Micah, came out on tour to share the stage. He was happy because he knew how happy that made Willie. I spoke about how he was especially proud of Micah, also a drummer and painter, and how proud he was to have an original Micah drawing hanging on the wall at home. I spoke about Paul's unbreakable bond with his brothers, his three boys, and his grandson. How he prized Billy's talent. How he relished RP's role as a writer and poet. How he rejoiced in Evan's intelligence and integrity. How he counted on Darrell Wayne's loyalty and love."

Janie went on to speak about Paul's spirituality.

"Although he veered from his father's Pentecostal path," she said, "he remained a believer. His favorite scripture was from James chapter 2: 'You see that a man is judged by works and not by faith alone.'"[9]

She summed it up beautifully.

"All of us gathered here today are a testament to Paul's good works and the amazing human being that he was. Everyone he met he made feel valued. When I look at the band Family, I know that his spirit is still out there on the road with you. We will love and miss him every day for the rest of our lives. He was a tough act to follow. In the words of another Willie, Shakespeare, 'He was a man, take him for all in all, I shall not look upon his like again.'"[10]

Amen.

The brood. From left to right:
Taylor (Evan's wife), Evan English, Paul, Willie, Paul "Trey" English III,
Paul English Jr., and Mandy English (Paul Jr.'s wife).

"ME AND PAUL"

It's been rough and rocky travelin'
But I'm finally standin' upright on the ground
After takin' several readings
I'm surprised to find my mind's still fairly sound

I guess Nashville was the roughest
But I know I've said the same about them all
We received our education
In the cities of the nation, me and Paul

Almost busted in Laredo
But for reasons that I'd rather not disclose
But if you're stayin' in a motel there and leave
Just don't leave nothin' in your clothes

And at the airport in Milwaukee
They refused to let us board the plane at all

They said we looked suspicious
But I believe they like to pick on me and Paul

Well it's been rough and rocky travelin'
But I'm finally standin' upright on the ground
And after takin' several readings
I'm surprised to find my mind's still fairly sound

I guess Nashville was the roughest
But I know I've said the same about them all
We received our education
In the cities of the nation, me and Paul

On a package show in Buffalo
With us and Kitty Wells and Charley Pride
The show was long and we're just sittin' there
And we'd come to play and not just for the ride

Well we drank a lot of whiskey
So I don't know if we went on that night at all
But I don't think they even missed us
I guess Buffalo ain't geared for me and Paul

Well it's been rough and rocky travelin'
But I'm finally standin' upright on the ground
And after takin' several readings
I'm surprised to find my mind's still fairly sound

I guess Nashville was the roughest
But I know I've said the same about them all
We received our education
In the cities of the nation, me and Paul

ACKNOWLEDGMENTS

More than anything I'd like to thank Paul English for the many years of love and loyalty.

—WILLIE NELSON

★

Thanks to Willie, Annie Nelson, Mark Rothbaum, David Vigliano, and my editors Andrea Fleck-Nisbet and Veronika Shulman. Special gratitude to Janie English, without whom this book wouldn't have been possible, as well as Paul's sons, Evan, RP, and Darrell Wayne, and his brother Billy. And, as always, my wife, Roberta, and my loving family and friends.

—DAVID RITZ

NOTES

1. Mark Twain, *Mark Twain's Notebook*, ed. Albert Bigelow Paine (New York: Harper & Brothers, 1935), 240.
2. "Absolutely Sweet Marie," track 11 on Bob Dylan, *Blonde on Blonde*, Columbia Records, 1966.
3. Samuel Taylor Coleridge, "The Rime of the Ancient Mariner," 1834, Poetry Foundation, poetryfoundation.org/poems/43997/the-rime-of-the-ancient-mariner-text-of-1834.
4. Kahlil Gibran, *The Prophet* (New York: Alfred A. Knopf, 1940), 19.
5. Gibran, 20.
6. Gibran, 15.
7. *Hamlet*, ed. Horace Howard Furness (Philadelphia: J. B. Lippincott, 1905), 1.5.166–67. References are to act, scene, and line.
8. Meagan Flynn, "Paul English, Willie Nelson's Best Friend, Drummer and Formidable Enforcer, Dies at 87," *Washington Post*, February 13, 2020, washingtonpost.com/nation/2020/02/13/english-willie-died.
9. Paraphrase of James 2:24.
10. *Hamlet*, 1.2.187–88.

ABOUT THE AUTHORS

WILLIE NELSON

is Willie Nelson, American icon and

winner of too many awards to mention.

★

DAVID RITZ,

author of sixty books, has worked with

everyone from Ray Charles to Don Rickles.